W9-CFG-403

To Jean Koefoed,
our hero

TABLE OF CONTENTS

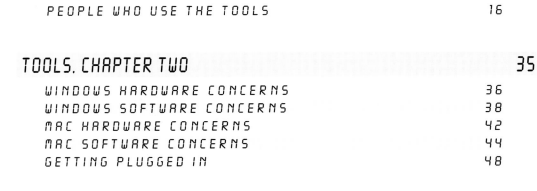

MANY
THANKS

We began playing with 3D on our personal computers back in the days of Super 3D and Swivel. As much as we would like to think that we were doing cutting edge stuff, the reality is that we were just playing. Six years ago, 3D still had a way to go. Today 3D is a serious growth industry. The job of computer animator is ranked number one by a *USA TODAY* poll on careers of the future in terms of employment growth numbers. In other words, 3D animation has arrived–big time.

This growth, much like this book, is possible because of the talented individuals who push the programs to the limits and the companies that generate reasonably priced animation programs.

Many individuals assisted in the birth of this book. First and foremost was the man who paved the way for our first book, *Animation and 3D Modeling on the Mac*, Jean Koefoed. His name is absent from the first book's acknowledgment page because he demanded that he not be mentioned. We are sure if he were alive today, he would demand the same of this book. We are hoping he will forgive us for bucking his wishes, but he deserves the recognition.

Jean died of cancer last summer, but he will be fondly remembered by us–and by many other authors in whose abilities he showed faith. Jean's life included saving the Jewish people through the Danish underground during WWII, pursuing a shared love of sailing, and serving as associate publisher of Print Books. My ears still ring with the words from Carmen, his wife, when I picked up the telephone: "Don, our hero is gone." We will miss you, Jean. Happy sailing.

The other visionaries who have guided and influenced this book are the 3D animators who are combine technical savvy with the visual arts. We would like to thank them for their help through the years and with–sometimes in an unwitting manner–help in providing concepts for this book. They include Chuck Carter, Bill Baker, Troy Benesch, Juan Thomassi, and Peter Kohama.

Over the years, we have dealt with almost all of the software companies that make 3D animation possible. They range from small, three-person shops and family operations to huge corporations. All of them create wonderful programs. We would like to thank the staffs at Adobe, Macromedia, Electric Image, Autodes-sys, Metacreations, Fractal Design, Questar Productions, Caligari, Sonic Foundry, Sound Ideas, Kinetix, Microsoft and Alien Skin Software.

To those who stood by us through this year of rapid change–which allowed us to laugh in the face of convention and gave us the moral and financial support, making this project possible–we would like to thank Ray and Carol Sumser; Bob and Linda Farley; Hal and Sandy Switzer; Stella and Nick Matalas; Nora and Hunter Jones; Jenny and Bill Reinhart; Kim and Don Witman; Chris Sloan, Hillel Hoffman, and Nick Karilloff at *National Geographic*; Bob Dick and Magdalena Alfaro at World Data; Paul Babb and Jay Roth at Electric Image; Jan Hirschfeld and Adam Konowe at the U.S. Chamber of Commerce; Dale Glasgow of Glasgow and Associates; Melissa Cronyn of the U.S. Parks Service; Chris Garcia of *Popular Science*; Susan Weissman of Northern Virginia Community College; and LaNeil Gregory of Hines Engineering.

At Graphic-sha we would like to thank Toshiro Kuze and Rico Komanoya, who have demonstrated faith in our abilities and let us work on this second book for them. We also thank Nancy A. Ruenzel from Peachpit Press who guided the English edition and our Peachpit editor Victor Gavenda who tossed in many great suggestions.

As corny as it sounds, we also thank you, the reader. Your e-mail from the first book gave us the inspiration to work on this book. We hope that many of your "How would you..." questions are answered. Much like the first book, we will do our best to answer any future questions that you have. Please visit our Web site, which will support the ideas and update the charts shown within this book.

don@foleymedia.com
http://www.foleymedia.com

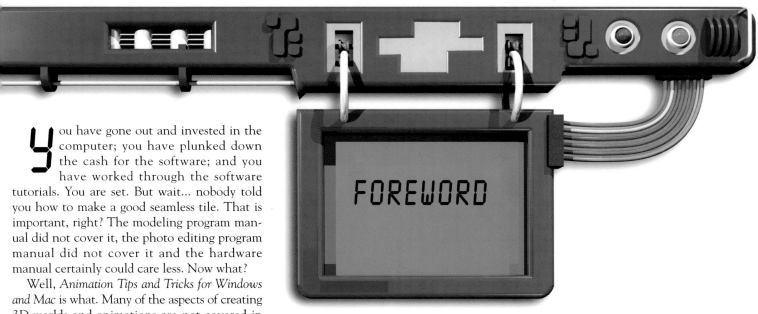

FOREWORD

Y ou have gone out and invested in the computer; you have plunked down the cash for the software; and you have worked through the software tutorials. You are set. But wait... nobody told you how to make a good seamless tile. That is important, right? The modeling program manual did not cover it, the photo editing program manual did not cover it and the hardware manual certainly could care less. Now what?

Well, *Animation Tips and Tricks for Windows and Mac* is what. Many of the aspects of creating 3D worlds and animations are not covered in manuals. The manuals do a good job of explaining how to use the program, but you are on your own after that. With a vivid imagination and a little common sense you can usually work your way through most hurdles. The building blocks are there. You just need to figure out how they fit together. While this discovery period can be a fascinating way to explore a new virtual world, sometimes it just leaves you smashing your head on your keyboard.

Designed to be used by both Windows and Macintosh users, the tips mentioned throughout the book can be applied to most any modeling, animation and editing programs. While users familiar with just one of those platforms may think this claim is a little far-fetched, those using both platforms can attest to the fact that both Windows and Mac work almost identically. Programs that are ported to each platform work with the same set of palettes and menu commands.

This book touches on thousands of possible effects that can be generated in the digital domain. It also creates a foundation which you can embellish and evolve to match your own needs and styles. Sometimes you will read something here that triggers an idea for adding that little flair to your production.

Packaged with *Animation Tips and Tricks* is a CD-ROM that can be read on both Windows and Mac machines. The CD-ROM contains many of the texture maps used to create the images in the book, a host of home-grown sound effects, an interactive gallery of the work of many animators and two dozen models in dxf format and a selection of background images for you to incorporate into your own productions.

No matter why you got into animation–for creating animated GIFs for your Web site or for developing animations for movies–you have most likely found that 3D animation work is more complicated than any other work you have tried on your computer. It is not an easy thing to build new worlds from scratch, and that is just what most 3D animation programs are capable of.

Learning to use 3D programs is difficult and even well-produced manuals fall short in helping to take you to the next step–what to do once you have learned the program. This book helps to guide you through some of the effects and techniques with which you will want to experiment as you grow with your software.

Do not be frustrated as you start. Most programs take months of regular use before the fundamentals of the software become second nature or even begin to make sense. You are facing a learning curve that you never had to deal with when learning a word processor or even a 2D drawing program.

It is worth the wait.

THINGS YOU
NEED TO KNOW
ABOUT THE BOOK

Generally, it is a good idea to run a strip of masking tape along the edge of a piece of wood when cutting it with a table saw. Doing this prevents splintering. While this may seem like a useful tip (if not entirely out of place in an animation manual), you will not find it in the manual that comes with the table saw. The table saw manual provides enough information to get the saw up and running– and it may provide a few useful tips– but it will not dwell on other matters of interest to users.

Software manuals often approach the world in a similar manner. They will do what they can to explain the functions of the program and perhaps provide useful tips, but to fully explore the world of possibilities the software can handle is not what the manual provides. Just as the table saw manual will not tell you how to build a house, the manual that came with your 3D program is not going to tell you how to build a skyscraper. But within these pages, you can learn how to build in 3D.

This cute little metaphor can be stretched in another direction. Once you have figured out how to use the saw, you might go out, buy a book on home projects, and decide to build a table. The book you buy on building a table gives you all the tips and tricks you need to know about how to build the table, including how you might use your saw. But the final project is not dependent on what kind of saw you use. Well, *Animation Tips and Tricks* does not care what kind of saw you have, nor does it care what program or platform you use. The tips outlined here are almost universally applicable to any 3D modeling environment. The concepts are important, not telling you what dialog box or menu option to choose. In the few instances when programs are men-

tioned specifically, such as After Effects, Photoshop, or Eye Candy, the programs are available for both the Windows and Macintosh platforms.

WHAT YOU NEED TO KNOW

To be able to use this book effectively you need to know how to use your 3D modeling and animation programs and your image- and video-editing programs. The book's scope is sharing concepts that help you develop special effects and interesting images for your production.

In the woodworking book example, you do not **have** to build its table. You can take from the instructions what you want and build your own custom table, making your table fit your needs. Amazingly enough (well, perhaps not that amazing), the idea is the same for the instructions you will find here. Sure, you can follow them exactly and come up with the same results, but more likely, you will want to expand on the concepts and adapt the ideas to your own projects.

THOUGHTS ON PLATFORMS

Once upon a time, users could take an elitist stance and declare that their platform was the best. ("DOS rules, the Mac is a toy.") This was usually based on some twisted techno-patriotism declaring one's home ground supreme (the ONLY platform for creativity is the Mac), and the other side was obviously inferior. Humankind has pretty much been doing this since we first learned to grunt, so it is not too surprising that the same thing would happen with computer platforms.

The reality is, there is not that much difference between the two anymore. Sure, the Mac had its lion's share of creative tools, but realizing that the overwhelming majority of desktop computer users were Windows-based, almost every creative tool found on the Mac eventually was cranked out on a Windows version. If you look down the list of top Mac 3D tools, you will find quality Windows brethren: Photoshop, Director, Electric Image, form•Z, After Effects, Metacreations, and more, all are available on both platforms and are equal in features and stability.

The result is two platforms with nearly the same creative content. In fact, a user creating animations in both platforms with the same product usually will find that they are identi-

cal–menu commands, features and even formats are almost always the same. A Mac user working in Photoshop can sit down at a Windows machine and not skip a beat. Every dialog box, menu item, and palette, while being slightly cosmetically different, are the same.

Animation Tips and Tricks was written with this in mind. All the techniques are applicable to both platforms.

WHAT TOOLS YOU SHOULD HAVE

Obviously you are going to need some kind of 3D program. Most programs allow you to build a model, apply textures, and animate and render the file. Some allow only portions of each of these functions. You will want to consider what features are important to your needs before you buy (see charts on pages 40-41 and 46-47 for more details).

You also will need a video or animation editing program. While you could survive without one and live with the direct output from your animation program, you really would be limiting yourself. Editing programs allow you to import multiple sequences, composite images, edit sounds and add special effects and all of these features are key to quality productions.

In addition, you will want a good image editing program for creating and editing texture maps and backgrounds. It is not hard to go out on a limb here and just tell you to buy Photoshop. You need it. While you can work with other programs such as xRes, the reality is Photoshop is the best all-around image editing tool and will be one of the most important programs in your toolbox. Photoshop is one of the few programs mentioned by name consistently through the Tips and Tricks section of the book. This is because Photoshop is such a natural choice for the tasks that need to be performed. You can perform the same techniques with other programs, but Photoshop is so popular, it is assumed that if you are dealing with animations, then you are working with Photoshop.

In a few cases, we mention programs like Eye Candy and Kai's Power Tools. These are great tools that can often provide quick ways of doing things that would take much longer to do from scratch. These programs are not required, but combined with other filter packages such as Paint Alchemy and Gallery Effects, they can add impressive weight to an animator's bag of tricks. This bag of tricks often can pull animators out of tight spots or creative barriers, so they are recommended.

HARDWARE REQUIREMENTS

Faster is better. Bigger is better. This boils

Both Windows and Mac platforms offer a strong variety–and almost identical–lineup of quality 3D products that range in cost to suit both amateur and professional needs. At a minimum, serious animators need at least three programs: an integrated modeling/animation/rendering package, a video/animation editing program and a photo editing package. The list of additional programs animators either will require or simply lust after include: a good set of filters for image and motion editing, sound editing tools, morphing and distortion tools, landscape and tree generation programs, and MIDI editing software.

down to buying a fast computer, lots of disk space and tons of RAM. In these days of doubling CPU speeds, it is silly to say what is the best system. The best system is the one that came out last week. A more realistic perspective can be seen from the minimum requirements.

While there is a little debate in what a minimum speed may be, you are inviting frustration if you try to work with anything under 75MHz. A few years ago, you may have been using a 33MHz machine for 3D work and it did just fine. However, the rest of the world leaped forward and so did the software. You will need to be working with a Pentium chip for Windows and a PowerPC chip for the Mac. The comfort range for most animation programs starts around 120MHz. Largely a matter of perspective, 120MHz is the point where you may not be pulling your hair out waiting for a simple wireframe screen to redraw. If you spent a week working on a 360MHz machine, you could never go back to 120MHz. If you worked with a 75MHz machine, 120MHz would seem like heaven.

All programs ship with minimum RAM requirements. Never, never look at these as a limitation on how much RAM you should buy. At a minimum, make sure your machine has twice the RAM listed as the highest minimum requirement of the tools in your toolbox. For example, Electric Image's minimum requirement is 32MB of RAM. Yes, you could run the program and create simple animations if you had 32MB of RAM, but that is about all. You really want at *least* 60MB RAM. Avoid all RAM doubling and virtual memory schemes. At best, they slow you down; at worst they cause you to crash.

OUTPUT DEVICES

If you are developing animations for CD-ROMs, kiosks or the Web, you can develop the final product all within your own computer. For in-house broadcast output, you need to have a hardware compression/decompression board. Yet creating broadcast animations does not require you to rush out and buy an expensive video output board. If you have access to a service bureau or post-production house, you

To create a vivid 3D world, you do not need tens of thousands of dollars or dedicated high-end rendering systems. All the animation images at right were created by Windows and Macintosh machines running at less than 150mhz with off-the-shelf software (Infini-D, form•Z, Electric Image) ranging from $400 to $3,000.

can output your files remotely by hauling a hard drive or a compact disk recorder (CDR) to the site. Most places charge a couple hundred dollars an hour for this service, so make a trip ahead of time to make sure your hardware and software is compatible. In some cases you might be able to use software compression on your animations that work with the site's system. If this is the case, you will save conversion time—and time is money.

If you are just starting out in animation and want to create animations for animation's sake, you can live with working within your computer and viewing your output on your monitor. Utilities such as Movie Player allow you to view small animations synchronized with audio on your screen. For playback, you also can import your animations into authoring programs like Director or editing programs like Premiere.

THE BOTTOM LINE

The hardware and software you need depends on what kind of animations you plan to produce and what kind of dedication you want to put into your animations.

If the sole purpose of your animations is to be small animated GIF files for a Web site, buying form•Z and the full film version of Electric Image would be overkill. In this instance, your modeling and animation needs are going to be simple, so integrated packages such as StudioPro, Infini-D and Ray Dream Designer will most likely suite your needs. If you are already working the Web, you probably already have Photoshop. Shareware utilities such as GIF Builder or the GIF Construction Set can turn your animation output into GIF files, so you are all set.

If you want to create complex, character-based animations for broadcast use, you will want a modeler (form•Z or Extreme 3D) to handle organic shapes, and a good animation program (Electric Image or Lightwave) to support inverse kinimatics. In addition, you will need a robust editing program (After Effects).

The contrast between animations for Web or broadcast shows the variety and cost contrasts of software programs available. On the less expensive end, you can get everything

you need for a couple hundred dollars (not including Photoshop because you are going to need it anyway), and on the high end, you can get what you need for a few thousand dollars.

For hardware, the best thing to do is to pay a little extra for a machine that allows you to upgrade the CPU. Things are changing so fast nowadays that you will be left in the computer middle ages within two years if you cannot keep up. This may mean that your computer may not be able to run as fast. But, in a more fatal scenario, you might not even be able to run future programs as operating systems quickly evolve to keep up with the pace.

The final decision on what you buy—once you get past all the features and options—always ends up at the same point. How much money can you spend? It really is a "you-get-what-you-pay-for" world. While going into debt to buy a computer system is not always a great idea, it is worse to buy a system that does not do what you want it to and ends up gathering dust because of its inability to perform. Bite the bullet, and pay what you can. It will be worth it down the road.

If you have not settled on a platform yet, you have the same concerns. The decision depends on what you want to do with the system. Then look at the programs available. For character animation, you might be more inclined toward Softimage, which has yet to come out on the Mac. Or you may be concerned with output needs. If you are working with Avid systems, you might lean toward a Mac for fewer translation hassles.

In terms of stability, no matter what each side says about the other, both platforms have evolved to incredibly stable animals, considering the number of crashes we had to deal with a few years ago. A properly configured system, no matter what the platform, can actually go on indefinitely without crashing. In the production of this book, not a single system error occurred on the Windows or the Mac platform. This goes a distance in declaring the stability of the systems, but it also says a lot about having adequate RAM and few third party startup programs running.

THE COMPLETE ANIMATOR'S STUDIO

Animations are seldom born completely out of a computer. The computer should be seen as a great meeting place for all the elements needed to create the final product. While an animator certainly can survive without leaving the digital realm of the computer, bringing in elements from the outside world and producing files that can be played back on a variety of mediums is half the fun. In addition to hardware and software choices (see Chapter 2), the items mentioned below could be viewed as a wish list, but for many animators, they represent minimum requirements.

CAMERA

A good 35mm camera will suffice. Using this tool is the first step for capturing high-quality images that can be brought into your computer. Your film can be processed and you can scan in your slides or prints; or you can have the local photo processor record the images on a Kodak CD-ROM so you can open them directly in Photoshop. One hour photo services make it possible to keep your creative juices flowing if you need to go out and shoot a picture of a cow or a tree after an inspirational thought.

If you have a digital camera, you are one step in the right direction. Using a low-cost digital camera is a quick way to get low-resolution textures, but you pay the price if you want higher resolution for objects close to the camera or for 3D work destined for the print world. More expensive digital cameras are wonderful–generally starting around $2,000–but out of the budget range for many.

SCANNER

Scanners have multiple uses. The most obvious is scanning photographs of textures or placing the texture objects right on the scanning bed and getting an instant texture map. Other great uses are scanning in floor plans to design buildings around an accurate template or scanning in maps to get precise topographical

Animators' studios are going to vary in the equipment they need depending on the kind of work they do. A well-rounded general purpose setup might include the following items:
1) a fast CPU with lots of RAM and a CD-ROM; 2) a main monitor no smaller than 17"; 3) a secondary monitor or an NTSC monitor; 4) a set of quality multimedia speakers; 5) a 35mm camera; 6) a camcorder; 7) a CD-ROM recorder; 8) a large capacity external hard drive; 9) removable media; 10) an audio CD/cassette source; 11) external sound devices; 12) a scanner; and last, but certainly not least, 13) software that allows you to build models, animate, render, edit, and produce your productions.

data for gray-scale terrain maps. If a scanner is not in the budget, you might want to check out your local parks department or community college education system. Many offer access to computer equipment labs for flat hourly fees, typically around $4.00 an hour. If they have a scanner, you can digitize a lot of photos for a small fee.

VIDEO CAMERA

Assuming you have video capture capabilities on your computer, you can use a video camera to capture low resolution images and to supply motion video backgrounds for compositing 3D images. Since you have instant feedback and little expense with videotape, it makes a great tool for research in the field. If you are building a city scape, you can walk around a city block and film lamp posts, newspaper boxes, parking meters and all the other little details. Back in your studio, you can refer to the tape for all the details and save yourself a trip back to the site. Hi-8 and SVHS tapes provide a higher quality capture than standard 8mm or VHS video recorders.

CD-ROM RECORDER

Video files are big and storage on even large-capacity hard drives seems minimal when dealing with animation files. One of the best ways around this is to keep your hard drive free for working files and save all your archive, model and texture files on CD-ROMS. (It is assumed that your computer has a CD-ROM player. If not, modern technology will cause you to struggle through life.) You can even create an "All of my favorite textures" CD-ROM that you leave in your machine when modeling. If the files are uncompressed, you can access them directly without eating up disk space by transferring them over.

You can store finished animation files on CD-ROM and send them to service bureaus for final output if you do not have a recording system. One of the perks is that you can master interactive CD-ROM productions that feature your animations by using authoring software such as Director.

REMOVABLE MEDIA

Zip, Jazz, SyQuest and other removable media have replaced floppy disks for multimedia developers. If you are lucky, you might be able to store one low-resolution texture on a floppy disk, but that is about all.

MODEM

A wealth of textures, models and sounds are available on-line. It would be a waste not to tap into this source. Most on-line services have animation forums where users share ideas and help solve problems. Software manufacturers now post drivers and upgrades online, saving time and money. The Web offers hundreds of sites for a variety of animation purposes, including textures and music tracks.

SOUND BOARD

Macs have sound input built in and most Windows sold today ship with sound boards. Make sure you can import audio with your board. You will use it for capturing audio. If you do not have 16MHz audio input, as Woody in the movie *Toy Story* said, "GET ONE!"

AUDIO DEVICES

Animations come to life with audio. You can buy CD-ROM soundtracks or you can input from devices such as microphones, cassette decks or keyboards. Even inexpensive keyboards ship with 128 voices and a large range of controls for sound effects. A good microphone (not the cheap one that came with the computer) allows you to add narration or foley effects (homemade sound effects, not related to the authors– but we do have some on the CD.)

If you want a model of a bagel to really look like a bagel, you need a bagel. The surface map for the bagel in this scene (above), as well as the newspaper, was obtained by scanning in real-world objects. Having a scanner in your studio is one of the best ways of bringing real-world elements into your digitized world.

ANIMATION IS
A MULTIMEDIA
EXPERIENCE

"Multimedia" is a great buzzword. As far as buzzwords go, the intermarriage between animation and multimedia is a two way street. Animations can be created in a vacuum, using only the animator's imagination. However, it is more likely that the animator draws from a whole world of sights and sounds and includes them into the final production.

Taking a closed door approach is tempting when creating an animation because it does not require anything other than the computer. One of the computer's greatest assets is how it has become the meeting place for a wide range of media. There is little reason why animators cannot use the computer as a melting pot for the elements around them, incorporating these elements into the animation.

The most obvious elements are textures and backgrounds that can be brought easily into the computer by using a scanner. Video cards that digitize clips allow for animated textures and for environments into which the animation can be keyed. Sound boards allow users to capture audio from a wide range of sources and include them into the production.

Even if an animator's creation is born and bred entirely in the computer, chances are that the concepts and visions developed have some real-world grounding. Just like the saying, "there is no novel that is truly fiction, because even fiction is drawn from real life exposures and experiences," animations—even fanciful ones—are born from the thoughts and experiences of the animator in the real world.

Tapping into these resources becomes second nature to animators. The creativity involved can be as twisted as literally scanning the floor to capture a great bump map from the carpet, to recording the sounds of jets taking off at an airport for use with an aviation animation.

One important element that animators can learn from real-world experiences is timing. The time it takes a car to roll to a stop in the real world is the same amount of time it takes a car to roll to a stop in the animated world. While everyone watching animations understands that the environment created is a computer simulation, they still expect the same rules to apply in timing. If real life rules do not apply, then the scene is questioned or rejected. Natural timing can be created by sitting in a chair and imagining the sequences, but solid results are obtained by observations.

The bottom line for creating realistic, believable animations is knowing what portions of the real world you need to incorporate into your work and make sure you set yourself up accordingly. Nothing stymies creativity more than having to stop in your tracks and run out to buy a new program or chunk of hardware. With a scanner, sound board, video digitizing card, and camcorder in hand, you can keep the creative ball rolling and experiment without limitations. Even if your real-world imports are not useful, sometimes they create foundations for the fanciful elements that you might be dreaming up.

In the same thought, textures exist all around us. When you are in the right frame of mind, you will begin to find yourself looking at the textures of objects and the structural devices used in buildings. You will pay more attention to colors and real-world lighting. No one needs to become a 3D photocopy machine. But by understanding these concepts and observing them, you will be able to create better animations.

One trick is to keep a sketchbook handy at all times. Access to notes on surfaces, shapes, facades and thousands of other assorted details allows you draw from these elements in creating animations. Reference books, such as the Visual Dictionary or even a Sears catalog, give you quick access to visual information that keeps the project rolling along.

Good animators are great sponges.

CHAPTER ONE

PEOPLE WHO USE THE TOOLS

3D animators tend to come in one of two shades of colors. Some are consummate animators who spend every waking moment of their lives creating animations for games, entertainment, or industry. The others are the artists and studios who tap into the power of animation to further their projects down some media pathway, then relegate the programs to the back burner until needed for another project.

The animators and artists featured on the following pages exist in both of these worlds. They are a unique group of individuals who have managed to combine both the skills necessary to create a beautiful image, and the skills needed to keep their computers running at peak performance with a myriad of new 3D tools that keep streaming down upon them.

One way or the other, they all tap into the powerful programs and the desktop computers that allow them to create worlds and images that previously existed only in their minds.

When you begin dealing with artists and the images they create, the age-old battle over which platform is the best begins to blur. It is the artist, not the computers, that make the difference. This is reflected in the following pages, which are a mixture of both Windows and Macintosh images. The amount of time spent on a project begins to make more of a difference than which computer program was used. Focus on detail is simply that, a focus on what makes an image work. Even the most expensive, feature-packed program cannot replace raw talent.

The use of 3D tools is wide-spread and now covers the same ranges as any traditional art arena, as well as a few not so traditional artistic realms such as medical visualization and courtroom re-enactment. 3D work continues to grow in its most visible incarnation such as feature movies, special effects, and, of course, the gaming world. In the less glamorous, but no less important world of production art, the power of 3D tools is a blessing. Illustrators can produce an image, have it shredded by a client, and quickly rebound by re-adjusting lights and models and perhaps tweaking the camera lens angle and position.

Using the same program, one animator can create a character animation for a television commercial while another animator could create a spinning logo for a Web site. Same tools, different needs and separate visions.

Desktop animation and the artists who sit behind the keyboards have gone through quite a revolution in the past 10 years. Keeping up with the new waves of tools and fierce competition between software vendors is a godsend to some and a source of incredible frustration for others. After all the hoopla, the final result is professional-level features widely available in most programs at extremely reasonable prices.

For whatever reason artists first sit down at a workstation to create the first animations, the results are always the same—a realization that the tools are available and the only limitation is themselves.

ORBCOMM DEPLOYMENT
Kevin Shawly
From an animation on the deployment of an Orbcomm satellite, the scene was built in form•Z. Animated and rendered in Electric Image.

EFORCE   *Greg Nevius*

This scene was created using a combination of trueSpace for the modeling and rendering. Photoshop was used for touch-up and color correction.

SOLAR MOWER   *Dennis Lowe*

From an animation explaining the Solar Mower concept. Built in form•Z; textures generated in Photoshop; rendered in Electric Image; and composited in After Effects.

INFERNO   *Robert Sharo*

This video frame was created in 3D Studio Max using Detailer. Composited in Speed Razor.

MEDUSA TEMPLE   *Troy Benesch*

The temple was built in StudioPro with figures generated in Poser. The entire scene was composited in Photoshop.

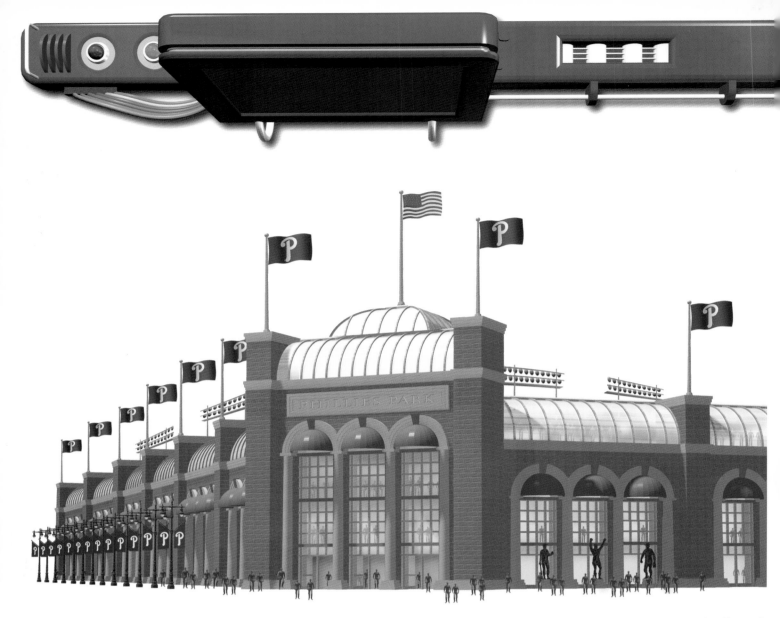

PHILLIES BALLPARK

Juan Thomassie

Short of actually constructing the building, few things beat 3D tools for architectural pre-visualization. This proposed design for the Phillies ballpark was created in form•Z and rendered in Electric Image. Tips on assembling buildings from scratch can be found on page 96.

BLACKBIRD

Juan Thomassie

With curves and odd surfaces, aircraft can be the most difficult and rewarding models to build. This aircraft was built in form•Z.

TIME CHANGE

Dennis Lowe

Detailed machinery and industrial engineering work hand-in-hand with programs such as form•Z. This scene was built in form•Z.

INDUSTRY

Greg Nevius

This scene was created using a combination of trueSpace for the modeling and rendering. Photoshop was used for touch-up and color correction.

UNDERGROUND NEW YORK

Don Foley

This illustration for *National Geographic* was created in Infini-D, using BackBurner to render the scene. The people were taken from digitized photographs and edited in Photoshop with motion blurs added to the people and train, as described on page 84.

PORSCHE BOXSTER *Troy Benesch*

The Porsche model was imported as a .dxf file from REM Infographica. The landscape was created in form•Z and rendered in Electric Image.

NY MEGAPROJECTS *Don Foley*

Constructed and rendered in Infini-D, this illustration for *National Geographic* used a texturing technique detailed on page 74.

OKLAHOMA BOMBING *Bill Baker*

The building was constructed in Infini-D and composited in After Effects. Tips for editing explosions can be found on page 62.

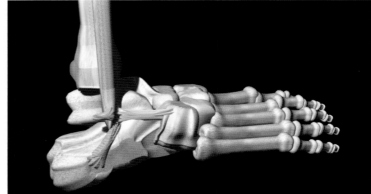

ANKLE BONES *Peter Kohama*

Medical illustration takes on a whole new photorealistic life when created with 3D tools. This foot skeleton was modeled in Infini-D, exported to Electric Image, and rendered using Photoshop textures.

ROBOT   *John Findley*

This scene was modeled and rendered in StudioPro. The surface maps were created in Photoshop. Some texture maps were imported from Pixar 128, others were created in Photoshop.

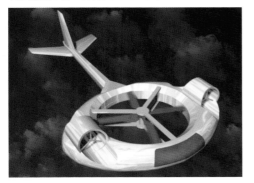

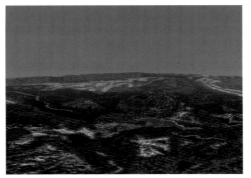

TRAFFIC ROBOT   *Dennis Lowe*

This animation was created in form•Z and textured in Photoshop. Animated and rendered in Electric Image.

DUSK   *Hans Westman*

The terrain in this scene was modeled in 3D StudioR2. The textures were created in Animator Pro.

EDEN   *Robert Sharo*

This video frame was created in 3D Studio Max using Detailer, and composited in Speed Razor.

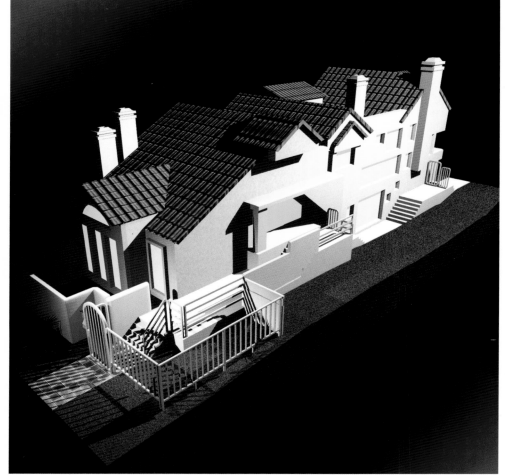

BROWN CONDO

Bill Baker

This crime-scene re-enactment was built in Infini-D and composited in Director. Photoshop was used to create the textures. Tips on constructing buildings can be found on page 96.

DECORATING DESIGN

Peter Kohama

Textured with Photoshop, this animation was built and rendered in Infini-D.

MITSUBISHI

Robert Sharo

This video frame was created in 3D Studio Max using Detailer, and composited in Speed Razor.

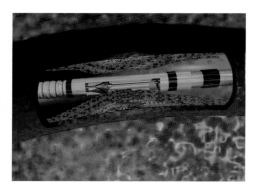

ATHERECTOMY

Peter Kohama

This medical animation was created, modeled, and rendered in form•Z.

HOUSE INTERIOR

Bill Baker

This animation was built in form•Z and rendered in Electric Image.

CASTLE DOOR

Sharkawi Che Din

This castle scene was modeled in form•Z and rendered in Electric Image.

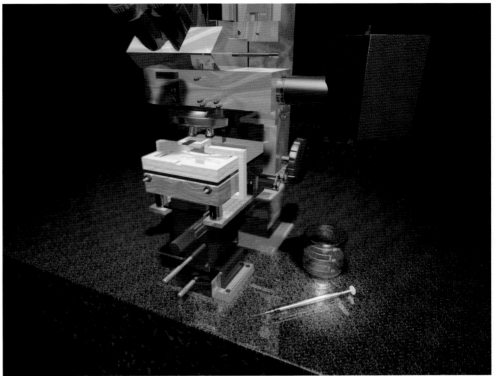

NBA PROMO *Dennis Lowe*

This broadcast logo was created in form•Z; textured in Photoshop; animated and rendered in Electric Image; and composited in After Effects.

MICROSCOPE *Shelly Green*

Modeled in form•Z, the file was imported into Cinema 4D for final rendering.

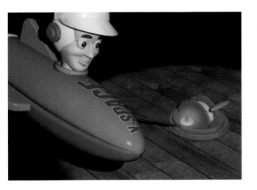

X-SPACE *Keith Carter*

Character animation is the focus of many artists in the field. This scene was modeled and rendered in Infini-D.

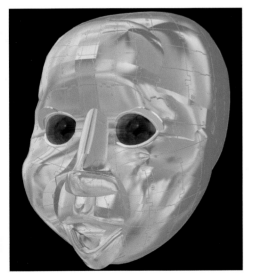

ASTONISHMENT *E.W. Parris*

Modeled in Infini-D, rendered in Electric Image.

MOUNTAIN POOL *Troy Benesch*

This montage has elements modeled in Strata StudioPro and images edited in Photoshop.

TATE BEDROOM *Amy Samelson*

This scene was modeled and rendered in Sculpt 3D. The final composition was done in Photoshop.

THANKSGIVING TURKEY *Peter Kohama*

Once challenging organic shapes are now simple fare. This turkey was created entirely in Infini-D with textures created in Photoshop.

SWING BRIDGE *Peter Kohama*

Photoshop textures were used in modeling this animation, built and rendered in Infini-D.

NO ESCAPE *Robert Sharo*

This video frame was created in 3D Studio Max using Detailer, and composited in Speed Razor.

CANDLES *Sharkawi Che Din*

The candles were created in Ray Dream Designer and rendered in Electric Image, with final composition done in Photoshop. For more on lens flares, see page 64.

NAVIGATING THE WEB

Don Foley

An illustration for *Newsweek*, the initial models were created in form•Z using a technique described on page 92 and rendered in Electric Image, with the earth image being edited into the scene using Photoshop.

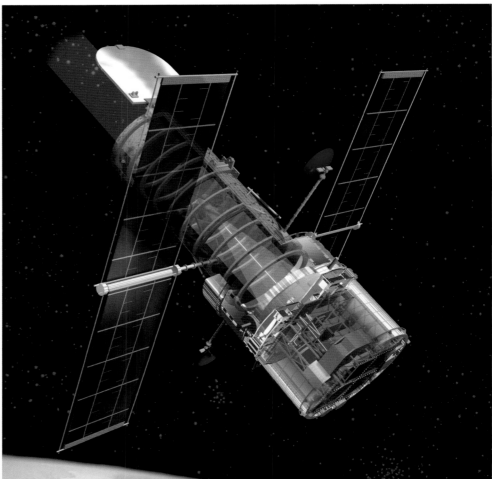

HUBBLE SPACE TELESCOPE *Don Foley*

The telescope and its innards were modeled in form•Z and rendered in Electric Image. The X-ray technique was composited in After Effects in a technique explained on page 60.

STAR WARS *Keith Carter*

Part of a trading cards series, this sequence was modeled using Infini-D and rendered using Electric Image.

CONQUEST *Robert Sharo*

This video frame was created in 3D Studio Max using Detailer, and composited in Speed Razor.

MKA *Kevin Cahill/Amy Samelson*

This lightscape scene was created for Mark D. Kruger Designs Light using Archicad, AutoCad and Lightscape.

BASKETBALL   *Juan Thomassie*

This basketball was created in form•Z; textured in Photoshop; and animated and rendered in Electric Image.

BUILDING   *Greg Nevius*

Bricks and mortar are one way to build a building; 3D tools are another. This scene was constructed in trueSpace.

OFFICE   *Advanced Graphic Applications*

This scene was created using AutoCad and rendered in Lightscape Visualization System.

HARRY SEILDER INTERIOR   *Amy Samelson*

This scene was modeled and rendered using Sculpt 3D.

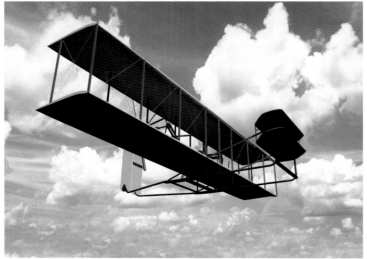

WRIGHT FLYER *Peter Kohama*

The scene from an animation was created and rendered in Infini-D with the final production being composited in After Effects.

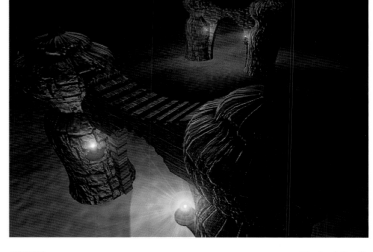

CASTLE *Sharkawi Che Din*

This study was created by a computer art major at Savannah College of Art and Design. It was modeled in form•Z and rendered in Electric Image.

FLOWER *Sharkawi Che Din*

The flower profile is a profile exported from Illustrator into form•Z, then textured and rendered in Electric Image.

LEHIGH VALLEY INTERNATIONAL *Kevin Cahill/Michelle Wilson*

Created for HNTB.Breslin Ridyard Fadero, this design of a satellite terminal was modeled in Archicad and Sculpt 3D on a Mac, and rendered in Lightscape on an NT machine.

PIANO *Robert Sharo*

This video frame was created in 3D Studio Max, using Detailer and composited in Speed Razor.

NAVY DEEP DRONE

Don Foley

This cover illustration for *Popular Science* was modeled in form•Z and rendered in Electric Image. Instead of using procedural shaders on the many small parts of the drone, which would make the craft seem like it was made of plastic, simple texture maps were used in a technique covered on page 124.

FLOWER *Peter Kohama*

This field was created in Infini-D; rendered in Photoshop; and composited for broadcast using After Effects.

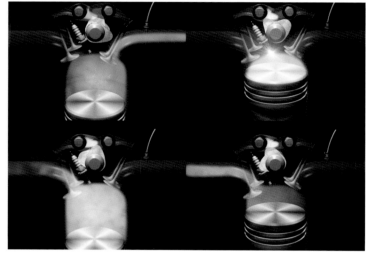

PISTON *Shelly Green*

These piston images were modeled in form•Z and rendered in Electric Image.

CAR *Shelly Green*

Modeled in form•Z and rendered in Electric Image.

ALCHEMY *Advanced Graphic Applications*

All the models in this scene were created using AutoCad and rendered in Lightscape Visualization System.

LABYRINTH *Frank Kanach*

This scene was built and rendered entirely in Bryce.

MARS MISSION   *Shelly Green*

These spacecraft images were modeled in form•Z and rendered in Electric Image.

MK-GOLD   *Advanced Graphic Applications*

This lightscape scene was created for Mark D. Kruger Designs Light.

CASTLE   *Advanced Graphic Applications*

This scene was created using AutoCad and rendered in Lightscape Visualization System.

OFFICE (View 1)   *Advanced Graphic Applications*

The models in this scene were created using AutoCad and rendered in Lightscape Visualization System. Using the same model, the camera's position was moved and an entirely new scene was rendered (*see OFFICE (View 2), below*).

OFFICE (View 2)

Advanced Graphic Applications

All the models in this scene were created using AutoCad and rendered in Lightscape Visualization System.

REENTRY   *Frank Kanach*

With final touch-up done in Photoshop, this image was built and rendered in Strata StudioPro.

LIGHT ANALYSIS   *AGA*

All the models in this scene were created using AutoCad and rendered in Lightscape Visualization System.

CAVE

Frank McIntyre

The scene's walls were created in Image2Mesh. The worm was created in form•Z. The entire scene was rendered using Electric Image.

LEK

Frank Kanach

The people in this scene were edited in Photoshop with the room being built and rendered in Strata StudioPro.

ULTHAR

Frank Kanach

The cat is introduced to the scene in post-Photoshop editing. The room was built and rendered in Strata StudioPro.

GLASS CLIFFS

Frank Kanach

This landscape was built and rendered entirely in Bryce.

SWEAZMOBILE
John Findley

This scene was modeled and rendered in StudioPro. The texture and surface maps were created in Photoshop. Some texture maps were imported from Pixar 128.

MYELIN
Shelly Green

The myelin cells were modeled in form•Z and rendered using form•Z's RenderZone module.

VAULT
Frank Kanach

Modeled and rendered in Strata StudioPro, this scene uses a gel on the light source to suggest the presence of bars.

ACCORDION
Marilynn DeSilva

Built and rendered in 3D Studio Max, this frame from an animation uses the Bones plug-in for motion.

MANHATTAN SKYLINE
Marilynn DeSilva

The undulating sheet was created in 3D Studio Max using deformation mapping.

CHAPTER TWO

WINDOWS
HARDWARE
CONCERNS

Both Windows and Mac platforms offer a strong various– and almost identical– lineup of quality 3D products. Costs range to suit both the amateur and professional. At a minimum serious animators need at least three programs: an integrated modeling/animation/rendering package, a video/animation editing program, and a photo editing package. Additional programs that animators either eventually will require or simply lust after include: a good set of filters for image and motion editing, sound editing tools, morphing and distortion tools, landscape and tree generation programs, and MIDI editing software.

If you are working with a Pentium-based system, you are going to want to run the Windows NT operating system. NT comes in two flavors: as a server operating system or as a workstation operating system. You want the workstation version.

Considered the Windows 95 for the business crowd, NT offers the same interface as its younger 95 brother, backed by a more robust operating system that is designed to handle serious applications like those used in 3D modeling and animation. The choice is not one of preference. Most of the packages available for animation require the NT operating system. While several programs, such as Ray Dream Designer, Photoshop, and Premiere, will run on a 95 machine, most of the higher-end animation programs, like 3D Studio Max, require NT. Programs designed for NT will not run on a 95 machine, yet most of the programs designed for 95 will run on an NT system. So when the dust settles and you are trying to decide what is best, NT is the way to go.

The biggest problem with NT is a small handful of support-type programs or non-animation related programs that still do not run on NT properly. This will change in the future (we hope) but it can be a hassle now. To resolve this issue, you may want to invest in a program called System Commander that allows you to run multiple operating systems on the same computer. While most 95 programs will run just fine on an NT system, it is nice to have the option if required.

While the introduction (page 8) outlined concerns and needs for animation in general, below are some items of note specifically for animators using a Windows system. The requirements for NT are pretty straight-forward. If you have adequate RAM, you will most likely be able to run NT on any machine that can handle Windows 95. The operating system will run on any 486, Pentium, or Pentium Pro workstation. While the operating system itself requires 12 megabytes of RAM, you should not go anywhere near a 3D application without at least 64 megabytes of RAM. Windows NT also operates on more sophisticated workstations, such as the Alpha.

The range of possibilities for a good, working animation system vary widely, here are a few things you need to observe while you are setting up your system.

THE BOX
You will need lots of slots to work in animation, so get a machine with at least six. Animation is a multimedia gig and you will find yourself filling up all the slots in a short time. With a modem card, a sound card, a SCSI card, an Ethernet card, and a video board you will fill up five slots. You may be tempted to save the space and money of buying a SCSI card by using your internal bus, but there are two good reasons that you may not want to install extra devices in your open bays. First, if your SCSI device, such as a second hard drive or an internal Zip drive has a problem, you will have some down time as you take apart your computer, or worse still, have the whole thing sent in for repairs. Second, if you are working with animation files, your output is going to be very large and having an external drive to simply unhook and transport is crucial.

THE PROCESSOR
Chances are you are going to spend a lot more money on software than you are hardware, so it would be silly to skimp early in the game and undercut yourself in terms of power. For a few hundred extra dollars you can hop from a machine running at 133mhz, to one based on 200mhz. If possible, buy a Pentium Pro workstation and consider a dual processor or at least dual-processing that can be upgraded for the future.

VIDEO BOARD
You are working in 3D, so at a minimum you are going to need a video board with 3D acceleration. Keep in mind that the board will only speed up screen redraw of 3D elements and not increase your rendering-to-disk time. As your

models get more complex, you will want the board to keep you working instead of spending your day waiting for the screen to redraw. A lot of inexpensive boards are available and many of these will do the job. Boards such as the Stealth 3D speed up redraw, game play, and serve as a general-purpose video board for all your non-3D work.

If you plan to output your own work to video you will need a video compression board on top of the video monitor board. Cards like the Perception Video Recorder board will eat up an additional slot, so make sure when you are buying you account for the growth.

RAM

Buy as much as you can afford. If you have four slots available you may want to load up as much as you can on two slots and leave two open for future expansion. Most new systems have RAM that is interleafed to increase speed. To take advantage of this, install RAM in pairs of identical chips: 64 megabytes is a starting point, 128 megabytes will keep you working steady without running into problems. Some programs, such as Softimage, require at least 64 megabytes of RAM, while most require at least 32 megabytes. Stay away from minimums though because it is nice to be able to run your modeling program and your image/texture editing program at the same time.

HARD DRIVES

If you plan on creating full screen animations, you are going to need serious disk space. Internal 3.2 gig drives are a nice place to start, but you will fill that up quickly. Get an external 2 gig drive so you can take your drive to a production house or client without too much hassle.

EXTERNAL MEDIA

Zip and Syquest drives allow extended flexibility in moving around large multimedia files and should be considered an important part of an animator's SCSI chain. A recordable CD-ROM drive can also be a life-saver, allowing for efficient back-ups and archiving of files that would otherwise use up a hard disk.

SOUND BOARDS

Windows machines do not come with built-in sound, so you will have to invest in a sound board. Get one that plays and records 16-bit sound (CD-ROM quality) and has gen-

eral MIDI capabilities. Most of the Sound Blaster boards available fall into this category.

If you are a former-Mac user working your way into the Windows world, you may find that the "plug and play" simplicity of a Windows machine is not the "plug and play" simplicity of the Mac. Newly installed hardware will need to be configured and compatible with all the possible hardware– a tenuous situation at best. Often, compatibility reports are available and some are even posted on the Web. It would be prudent to check around before investing in a new chunk of hardware.

Many companies will configure a system to your needs when you buy it. Since they have done all the configuring and checking of compatibility, this is a pretty smart way to go. When you expand with new boards at a later time, you may want to give the company that compiled your system a call and find out what kind of boards they use in their configuration when they assemble a new system. This cuts down on the guesswork involved.

Most workstations come as a bare box. As features are added, slots are used. Invest in a machine with room to grow. A machine with six slots gives most animators the space needed. A look inside the NT workstation below shows the slots fill up quickly when you are fulfilling just the basic needs, such as 1) modem board, 2) Ethernet adapter, 3) sound board, 4) video board, and 5) a SCSI adapter board.

WINDOWS SOFTWARE CONCERNS

Not too long ago, working with Windows to create animations was just a little bit daunting. While programs like 3D Studio offered impressive power, the DOS interface was anything but friendly and the number of supporting programs was inadequate. Things have changed. Interfaces for older programs have been updated, the NT operating system adopted the Windows 95 interface, and a host of new programs have either been newly developed or ported over from other platforms.

Almost every graphics and animation tool for the Mac, once the only place with a suite of tools to get the creative job done, has ported over to Windows. Some heavy-swingers like Softimage and Lightwave ported over from the SGI and Amiga lines. Backed up by powerful support programs such as Photoshop and After Effects, the Windows NT platform has become a merger of all the best of the available platforms mish-mash.

The spread of animation programs is wide, ranging everywhere from the lower-end Ray Dream Designer to the top-notch Softimage. In between can be found a healthy supply of middle range, multiple-purpose 3D animation programs such as trueSpace, Extreme 3D, Infini-D and Strata StudioPro, with 3D Studio Max edging to the top off the pile, but still affordable to the serious animator.

When it comes to formats, AVI (Video for Windows) is still the standard animation output with more programs offering support for QuickTime for Windows. Both formats offer compression based on installed CODECS, ranging from a lossless format at 100 percent quality to the Cinepak compressor for Web and CD-ROM work. As always, it is best to work at the highest possible quality until your final animation output. Usually, you will have the option to output as a sequence of TIF or Targa files. While this route will not support audio edits you may have generated with your animation, you will have the benefit of opening the individual files in Photoshop.

If you need to bounce between AVI and QuickTime formats, a shareware program called AVI/QT can be found on the Web. This program offers translation for going in either direction. No matter what compression you use, keep in mind that if you use a custom compressor (that is not shipped with the usual compressors), you will need to make sure your audience has access to that compressor.

Old timers from the DOS world running Windows NT will find an easy-to-use interface. Mac converts will find that NT offers many of the same navigational and menu offerings found in the Macintosh operating system. Many Mac programs have ported over to Windows such as Premiere, shown here with Studio Max.

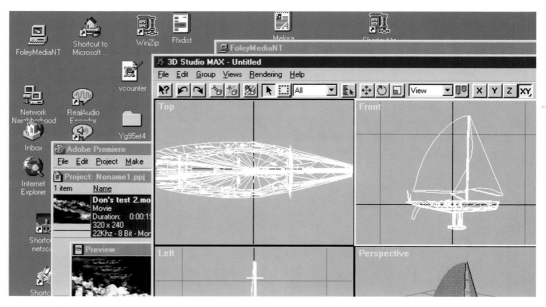

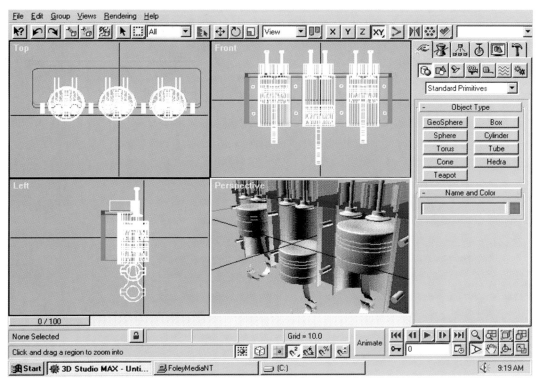

Programs like Studio Max, left, offer the simplicity of a graphical user interface with all the punch of a professional-level animation system.

Still-image formats for modeling programs import commonly used formats such as Targa and TIF. If you are working in another format that is not supported, Photoshop will be able to do a quick translation into either of these formats. DeBabelizer also can be used to convert files.

Model formats usually swing between either the native format of the program in use or .dxf, the AutoCad format that is the industry standard for both Windows and Macintosh platforms.

The trickiest thing about working in the Windows world is the huge variety of machines within which the software can run. Considering the hundreds of PC models available, the 3D applications you will be running are pretty stable. The first concern is to make sure you have adequate RAM to run your program, followed by support by the varying processors and accelerator boards available. While compatibility may seem like a nagging issue with Windows, it really is the result of a platform that gives you a greater number of options with a larger number of vendors, both of which help keep the costs of the systems reasonable.

Unlike other platforms where you might consider the hardware first and then get the software, with Windows you might want to look at it in the opposite light. Buy the software you want and tailor your hardware system around the program(s), configuring the 3D accelerator boards, RAM needs, and processor chip(s) to run in the most efficient and reliable manner. Going this route is not mandatory, but since your options are greater with PC setups, it gives you the opportunity to custom design your system. With a Macintosh system, for instance, many of your choices have already been made for you with the Power PC chip-of-the-moment, built-in sound, video, and a limited number of 3D accelerator boards.

If you would rather just buy your computer at the local appliance store, most programs will run just fine, given a reasonable RAM upgrade. Some programs, like 3D Studio Max, have a hardware key that hooks up to the parallel port, but you would be hard pressed to find a PC that did not have the parallel port to tap into.

The offerings for Windows platform animation tools have exploded in the past year as software companies that had products in the Macintosh, SGI, and Amiga platforms ported over to this popular platform. Almost every Macintosh player ported a version over to Windows 95 or Windows NT, boosting not only the number of animation programs available, but also supplying the important support programs such as Photoshop, After

Modeling and animation tools	Program's place in the world	What the program does well
3D Studio Max	All-purpose modeling, animation and rendering system	Affordable, well-rounded animation system
trueSpace	All-purpose modeling, animation and rendering system	Affordable, well-rounded animation system
Electric Image	All-purpose modeling, animation and rendering system	Powerful modeler and fast, realistic rendering
form•Z	Modeling and still rendering	Powerful, full-featured modeler
Infini-D	All-purpose modeling, animation and rendering system	Affordable, well-rounded animation system
Strata StudioPro	All-purpose modeling, animation and rendering system	Affordable, well-rounded animation system
Extreme 3D	All-purpose modeling, animation and rendering system	Affordable, well-rounded animation system
Ray Dream Designer	All-purpose modeling, animation and rendering system	Inexpensive, entry-level program
Bryce	Landscape creation, animation and rendering	Easy to use, fun interface
World Construction Set	Landscape creation, animation and rendering	Fantastically realistic landscapes
Poser	Human form modeling, animation and rendering	Completely editable and positionable human forms
Lightwave 3D	All-purpose modeling, animation and rendering system	Great character animation tools
Softimage	All-purpose modeling, animation and rendering system	Fantastic organics and motion control

Editing and 2D animation tools		
Photoshop	All-purpose image editing	Powerful tool set, best available on any platform
xRes	All-purpose image editing	Solid feature set
Media Paint	QuickTime painting and editing	Touch up and add effects after rendering
Illuminaire	2D animation and animation editing	Powerful 2D editing capabilities
After Effects	2D animation and animation editing	Powerful 2D editing capabilities
Premiere	2D animation and animation editing	Easy to use A/B video editing
Convolver	Creative filter effects palette	Powerful creative palette editing
DeBabelizer	Batch editing and filtering	Batch animation editing and translation
Speed Razor	2D animation and animation editing	Powerful 2D editing capabilities

Multimedia creation tools		
Director	Interactive multimedia development	Powerful capabilities via lingo scripting
mTropolis	Interactive multimedia development	Easy to use object-oriented creation

Support programs and plug-ins		
Eye Candy	Photoshop filter effects	Time-saving filters
Kai's Power Tools	Photoshop filter effects	Creativity-boosting filters
Morph	2D motion and still morphing	Easy-to-use morphing capabilities
Goo	2D warping	Just plain fun
Sound Forge	Audio editing	A whole audio editing studio in one box
Detailer	3D model texture creation	Paint on a model in a 3D environment
Artifex	Electric Image plug-in set	Bounce particle effects, lightning and more

Effects and Detailer. Most programs are designed to run smoothly on Windows NT, seen as the choice operating system for PC-based animators. Once seen as only serious business machines, PCs have moved quickly to support powerful graphic applications. The chart below reflects change as programs are added, dropped or evolve. This chart can be found on the Web at http://www.foleymedia.com/tips.

Tools	Platforms available	Great application for animators	Who needs it
3D Studio Max	NT	High quality modeling and animation	Studio and broadcast animators
trueSpace	95, NT	Solid, easy-to-use modeling and animation	Studio and broadcast animators
Electric Image	NT, Mac	Fantastic animations for video and film	Any animator looking for professional results
form•Z	NT, Mac	Detailed, precise modeling applications	Architects and industrial animators
Infini-D	95, NT, Mac	Quick, painless modeling, good for stills and Web work	Studios with multiple 3D needs
Strata StudioPro	95, NT, Mac	Quick, painless modeling, good for stills and Web work	Studios with multiple 3D needs
Extreme 3D	95, NT, Mac	A nice modeling toolkit for organic shapes	Studios with multiple 3D needs
Ray Dream Designer	95, NT, Mac	Entry level animators and the occasional 3D image	Students and studios with limited 3D needs
Bryce	95, NT, Mac	Backgrounds and environments	Anyone with landscape concerns
World Construction Set	95, NT, Mac	Backgrounds and environments	Anyone with landscape concerns
Poser	95, NT, Mac	Populating animations with small figures	Anyone dealing with human forms
Lightwave 3D	NT, Mac	Character animation	Studios with multiple 3D needs
Softimage	NT	Top-notch modeling and animation	High-end 3D animation studios

Editing and 2D animation tools

Photoshop	95, NT, Mac	Texture and background editing	Everyone
xRes	95, NT, Mac	Texture and background editing	Everyone else
Media Paint	95, NT, Mac	Adding special effects to finished animations	Those wanting to add artistic effects to animations
Illuminaire	95, NT, Mac	Compositing animations and other elements	Anyone creating final complex animations
After Effects	95, NT, Mac	Compositing animations and other elements	Anyone creating final complex animations
Premiere	95, NT, Mac	Editing between animation clips	Those mixing animations and video
Convolver	95, NT, Mac	Eye catching effects for still and video	Anyone interested in artistic palette shifting
DeBabelizer	95, NT, Mac	Processing finished animations	Anyone not living in a vacuum
Speed Razor	95, NT	Compositing animations and other elements	Anyone creating final complex animations

Multimedia creation tools

Director	95, NT, Mac	Creating complex multimedia and shockwave files	Serious multimedia developers
mTroplis	95, NT, Mac	Creating interactive productions	Serious multimedia developers

Support programs and plug-ins

Eye Candy	95, NT, Mac	Texture map creation	Modelers making texture maps
Kai's Power Tools	95, NT, Mac	Texture map creation	Modelers making texture maps
Morph	95, NT, Mac	Subtle shifts in object surfaces	Those with morph-shifting needs
Goo	95, NT, Mac	Bulging and warping post-rendered objects	Nobody, really, but it's nice to have in case
Sound Forge	95, NT, Mac	Editing sound effects for animations	Anyone who wants to add sound to animations
Detailer	95, NT, Mac	Accurate and straightforward texture application	Modelers looking for realistic surfacing
Artifex	NT, Mac	Creating fire, smoke, water and other fluid things	Animators in need of collision detection particles

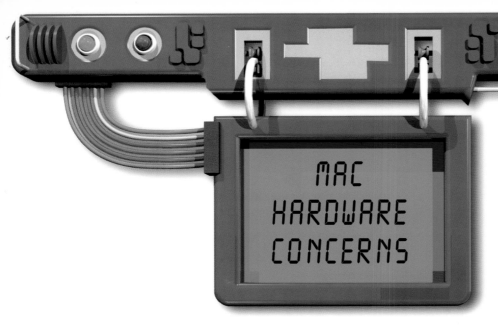

MAC HARDWARE CONCERNS

Building an animation system based on the Macintosh platform is a pretty painless experience. Straight out of the box, most medium- to higher-end Macs seem pre-configured for animation work. For instance, the 8500 series comes with built-in video support to drive a 17" monitor in millions of colors, 16-bit sound output, built-in SCSI connection, and Ethernet connectors. This leaves the machine's three PCI (peripheral component interconnect) slots available for focus on 3D applications, such as accelerators or video compression boards. Even modem support is supplied via a serial connection so no slots are used with a modem board. The system even includes NTSC video input and output that, while certainly not broadcast quality and supported only by software compression, serves as reasonable proofing output.

No matter what Mac system you end up with, you need to be based in the PowerPC world. If you are considering buying a used Mac for 3D work, keep in mind that some programs will not even run on the old 68X00 machines. Many programs may offer support for older Macs, but rendering times will be painful. Unless you are really on a tight budget and plan on doing low-end animation for the Web, invest in a PowerPC.

One of the biggest frustrations is buying the best computer on the market and finding it replaced by a newer, hotter model within a few months. In reality, Apple releases a new model every six months, so in even the best case scenario you are going to be left in the dark six months from now. Get used to it. In some instances, upgradable daughterboards are offered to replace the processing chip on the motherboard. These offer only temporary patches, as the true speed improvements in the future will not be based solely on how fast the chip runs, but how fast the machine's architecture will be to keep up with the chip. Buy a machine that will do the job at hand, with some hope of upgrading in the future. Then prepare for the announcement in the next week or two that a new Mac will soon be released, blowing the doors off the one you own. One benefit of this turnover is that shortly before new models are released, the prices of the current line are always slashed and you can pick up some great bargains—if you are willing to own dated technology.

The Macintosh offers a true plug-and-play architecture. In many cases you do not even need to load the drivers to the scanners, hard drives, and boards that are shipped with the product to make them work. While not loading the drivers is not suggested, it does show the power of compatibility the Mac offers.

One of the nicer Mac aspects is that you can plug a second video board into your machine and have a two-screen system that makes working with animations a dream. The two-screen system allows you to use one screen as a stage for your current working image or animation file and the second screen for the pile of tool palettes that most programs use.

Macintosh clones offer stable support for the same operating system and programs that Apple machines offer, often at very reasonable prices. The bottom line for most buyers is whether you get the slightly more powerful clone for the same cost of a Macintosh. Most

The Macintosh supports multiple screen displays, extending the animator's work real estate. With a two-screen system, one screen can be used as a stage and the second for tool palettes, as shown below. When creating models one screen can be used as a camera view and the other can be used for a three-window scene display.

The back of an 8500 shows the support built into some Macs, saving the internal slots for dedicated tasks such as 3D accelerators and video compression boards. Ports available include those for 1) video display, 2) NTSC input and output, 3) 16-bit sound input and output, 4) Ethernet connections, 5) SCSI chain connection, and 6) serial ports for printers and modems, as well as local talk network connection.

animators still stick with Apple's computers for fear of any surprise incompatibilities popping up on deadlines. While these fears may be unfounded, too many computers seem to operate on some black science and strange things happen all the time. Working with an Apple gives you one less thing to blame, leaving you to find another reason to explain the little mysteries that occur.

One upgrade you will want to make on your Mac is the RAM upgrade. No 3D program on the market is going to work well with the amount of RAM that ships from the factory. While some even go as high as 32 MB of RAM, you are going to need at least 100 MB to do any serious work. Programs like Electric Image need enough RAM to run both the program and the background Camera application to do test renders without leaving the main application. When working with modeling and animation programs, you most likely will want to run Photoshop at the same time

to tweak texture maps without quitting out of programs. Even running Photoshop by itself can be demanding on a computer's RAM. While it does use a temporary RAM disk cache, this slows things down so you want to allocate as much RAM to Photoshop alone. To be able to juggle the host of programs you will need to create animations, you should consider the 200 MB range for your RAM.

A large external drive is also a requirement for broadcast animation work. This gives you more space to work with and also allows you to transport your drive to a service bureau for output. You can usually just plug a drive on the end of your SCSI chain without loading any drivers and be off and running. Make sure it has its own SCSI identification and is terminated properly. Many drives on the market come with built-in terminators that can be toggled on and off. This is a good way to move drives around without too much hassle.

MAC SOFTWARE CONCERNS

Since the days of Swivel and Super 3D, the Mac has come a far way in terms of selection and quality of animation tools. Some of those tools produce animations for both Hollywood and broadcast TV. Not bad considering that those days were only six years ago.

The advantage of working with animation on the Mac is the fluid way that the host of programs available work together. It may seem to the user that many programs are simply modules of the same animation system, even though they are made by separate companies.

The beginning point of this conceptual animation system is often the image editing system. Photoshop, the current king of the image-editing hill; Painter; and Xres all offer solid support for texture creation. Working within these program's plug-in packages like Kai's Power Tools or Gallery Effects extend the creative possibilities even further.

When you hit the model creation portion of the project, you can choose from a dedicated modeling system like form•Z or an integrated package like Strata StudioPro. You can even mix and match platforms and build a model in Extreme 3D and bring an export of the file into Infini-D for animation and rendering.

This kind of flexibility allows the user to pick the best features from each modeler and apply them for the task at hand. It is nice to have a program like form•Z on hand for importing and exporting files. Even if you do not use the program for modeling, it serves as a good tool for filtering files. For example, you may buy or find a .dxf model to use in an animation, but have problems reading the file, or notice that polygons in the model are tweaking out for some reason or another. By bringing the file into form•Z and adjusting the export settings to something more compatible to you can often keep a project rolling with limited frustration.

If you do not live in the kind of world that affords you to buy a handful of modeling programs, several quality integrated systems are

Both Mac and Windows platforms offer a strong variety and an almost identical lineup of quality 3D products that range in costs that suit both the amateur and professional. At a minimum serious animators need at least three programs: an integrated modeling/animation/rendering package, a video/animation editing program, and a photo editing package. Electric Image, shown here, is a powerful animation package designed to meet the needs of both novice animators and high-end studios.

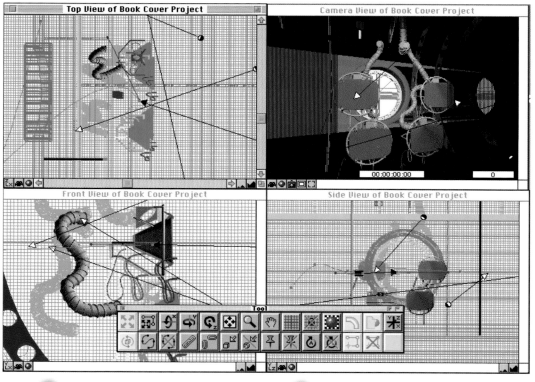

available with price ranges to fit almost any budget. For example, Ray Dream Designer, Strata StudioPro, Infini-D, Extreme 3D, and Electric Image all offer modeling capabilities combined with animation and rendering engines. The prices range from $200 to $3,000 with most of the mid-level packages falling in the $500 price range.

The bottom line when creating powerful images is not the software. While a better choice of tools will most certainly make your life easier, the true quality of the image depends on user talent. An animator with vision and imagination can create a more compelling animation with Ray Dream Designer than a hack with Electric Image. On the other hand, the same gifted individual with Electric Image is going to be a lot happier with a program that suits the needs of the project at hand.

When choosing a suite of tools, you will want to consider how they work together. The still-infant 3D metafile format should go a far way in the future to help iron out format incompatibilities between programs. The goal of the metafile format will be that any models and their associated textures will be able to be imported and exported from a range of modeling and animation tools without having to map the textures or have any incompatibilities with the model format. In a perfect world, you will be able to build a model in Strata StudioPro, import it into Detailer, paint directly on the surface, and ship the resulting file to Electric Image—all within the same 3D metafile format. While you can do this now, it really requires saving the file as a variety of formats and still mapping the final result at the end. Future implementations of 3D metafile will keep the creative juices flowing.

Formats between animation programs on the Macintosh are pretty standard. QuickTime support is pretty universal between all programs. If you save with the NONE codec or the ANIMATION codec at 100 percent quality, you will be able to work in a lossless mode and produce animations as sharp as any SGI system. If you have to have some compression for the final product, save it for the last step.

PICT sequence and PICS files are still supported by many programs and still have their place in the world. The biggest advantage of working with PICT sequences is that it is sim-

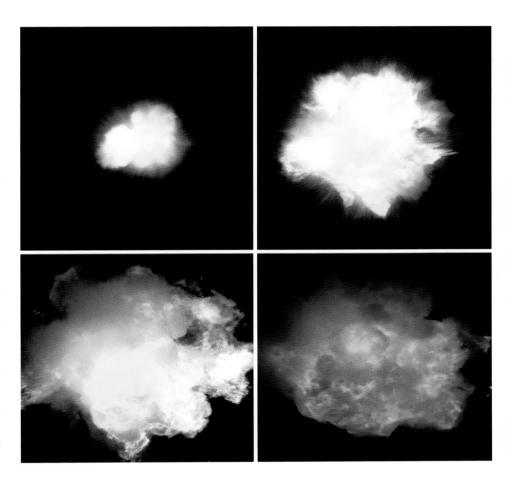

ple to open a single frame of an animation and tweak it in Photoshop. Both formats offer the advantage of being lossless. For still images, PICT files are still ahead of the pack, being a straightforward universal way to save all your texture maps. All 3D programs for the Mac offer PICT file import and all the editing programs allow for PICT import for art elements and backgrounds.

Even with this short list of simple palettes working universally on the Mac, it is a good idea to have a program like DeBabelizer on hand. Not only is it good for batch-editing animation files, it also serves as a good filter for transporting files. The occasional client may come up with a Targa file that you will need as a template or a background, and DeBabelizer makes short work of the conversion. If you are working on the Web, you will want to tap into DeBabelizer's optimization capabilities for fine tuning animations and still images to get them as small as possible without looking like mud.

Half the fun of creating animations is not using the programs themselves, but the support applications and resources available. Above are a few frames from Artbeat's ReelExplosions. Artbeats provides a series of digitized effects saved as both QuickTime and Targa formats in D1 (720x486) resolution. Where applicable, mattes are provided for composing.

The Macintosh software world is always evolving and expanding, so we will not even try to represent all the programs on the market. What we do present on the chart below are some of the key programs used by anima- tors to create professional animations for both broadcast and video uses. One of the most frequent questions is, "What software do I need?" To aid in answering this question, the chart below lists the programs, what they

Modeling and animation tools	Program's place in the world	What the program does well
Electric Image	All-purpose modeling, animation, and rendering system	Powerful modeler and fast realistic rendering
form•Z	Modeling and still rendering	Powerful full-featured modeler
Infini-D	All-purpose modeling, animation, and rendering system	Affordable well rounded animation system
Strata StudioPro	All-purpose modeling, animation, and rendering system	Affordable well rounded animation system
Extreme 3D	All-purpose modeling, animation, and rendering system	Affordable well rounded animation system
Ray Dream Designer	All-purpose modeling, animation, and rendering system	Inexpensive entry level program
Bryce	Landscape creation, animation, and rendering	Easy to use, fun interface
World Construction Set	Landscape creation, animation, and rendering	Fantastically realistic landscapes
Poser	Human form modeling, animation, and rendering	Completely editable and positionable human forms
Lightwave 3D	All-purpose modeling, animation, and rendering system	Great character and animation tools
Editing and 2D animation tools		
Photoshop	All-purpose image editing	Powerful tool set, best available on any platform
xRes	All-purpose image editing	Solid feature set
Media Paint	Quicktime painting and editing	Touch up and add effects after rendering
Illuminaire	2D animation and animation editing	Powerful 2D editing capabilities
After Effects	2D animation and animation editing	Powerful 2D editing capabilities
Premiere	2D animation and animation editing	Easy to use A/B video editing
Convolver	Creative filter effects palette	Powerful creative palette editing
DeBabelizer	Batch editing and filtering	Batch animation editing and translation
Multimedia creation tools		
Director	Interactive multimedia development	Powerful capabilities via lingo scripting
Apple Media Tool	Interactive multimedia development	Easy to use object-oriented creation
mTropolis	Interactive multimedia development	Easy to use object-oriented creation
Support programs and plug-ins		
Eye Candy	Photoshop filter effects	Time saving filters
Kai's Power Tools	Photoshop filter effects	Creativity-boosting filters
Morph	2D motion and still morphing	Easy to use morphing capabilities
Goo	2D warping	Just plain fun
Tree Professional	Tree creation	Design any tree to your specs
SoundEdit/Deck II	Audio Editing	A whole audio editing studio in one box
Final Effects	Animated effects for Premiere and After Effects	Dramatic and powerful effects over time
Detailer	3D model texture creation	Paint on a model in a 3D environment
Artifex	Electric Image plug-in set	Bounce particle effects, lightening and more

do, what animators can do with them, and who uses the programs. While a book cannot keep up with the growth in the field, a World Wide Web site can. The chart below can be found on the Web at http://www.foleymedia.com/tips, reflecting change as programs are added, dropped, or evolve.

Tools	Platforms available	Great application for animators	Who needs it
Electric Image	Mac, NT	Fantastic animations for video and film	Any animator looking for professional results
form•Z	Mac, 95, NT	Detailed, precise modeling applications	Architects and industrial animators
Infini-D	Mac, 95, NT	Quick, painless modeling, good for stills and Web work	Studios with multiple 3D needs
Strata StudioPro	Mac, 95, NT	Quick, painless modeling, good for stills and Web work	Studios with multiple 3D needs
Extreme 3D	Mac, 95, NT	A nice modeling toolkit for organic shapes	Studios with multiple 3D needs
Ray Dream Designer	Mac, 95, NT	Entry level animators and the occasional 3D image	Students and Studios with limited 3D needs
Bryce	Mac, 95, NT	Backgrounds and environments	Anyone with landscape concerns
World Construction Set	Mac, 95, NT	Backgrounds and environments	Anyone with landscape concerns
Poser	Mac, 95, NT	Populating animations with small figures	Anyone dealing with human forms
Lightwave 3D	Mac, NT	Character animation	Studios with multiple 3D needs

Editing and 2D animation tools

Tools	Platforms available	Great application for animators	Who needs it
Photoshop	Mac, 95, NT	Texture and background editing	Everyone
xRes	Mac, 95, NT	Texture and background editing	Everyone else
Media Paint	Mac, 95, NT	Adding special effects to finished animations	Those wanting to add artistic effects to animations
Illuminaire	Mac, 95, NT	Compositing animations and other elements	Anyone creating final complex animations
After Effects	Mac, 95, NT	Compositing animations and other elements	Anyone creating final complex animations
Premiere	Mac, 95, NT	Editing between animation clips	Those mixing animations and video
Convolver	Mac, 95, NT	Eye catching effects for still and video	Anyone interested in artistic palette shifting
DeBabelizer	Mac, 95, NT	Processing finished animations	Anyone not living in a vacuum

Multimedia creation tools

Tools	Platforms available	Great application for animators	Who needs it
Director	Mac, 95, NT	Creating complex multimedia and shockwave files	Serious multimedia developers
Apple Media Tool	Mac	Creating interactive productions	Presentation based developers
mTropolis	Mac, 95, NT	Creating interactive productions	Serious multimedia developers

Support programs and plug-ins

Tools	Platforms available	Great application for animators	Who needs it
Eye Candy	Mac, 95, NT	Texture map creation	Modelers making texture maps
Kai's Power Tools	Mac, 95, NT	Texture map creation	Modelers making texture maps
Morph	Mac, 95, NT	Subtle shifts in object surfaces	Those with morph-shifting needs
Goo	Mac, 95, NT	Bulging and warping post-rendered objects	Nobody, really, but it's nice to have in case
Tree Professional	Mac, 95, NT	Building complex trees painlessly	Architecture and animators creating outdoor scenes
SoundEdit/Deck II	Mac, 95, NT	Editing sound effects for animations	Anyone who wants to add sound to animations
Final Effects	Mac, 95, NT	Adding particle and light effects to animations	Animators wanted to add spot-render particle effects
Detailer	Mac, 95, NT	Adding realistic little details to models	Animators concerned with realistic texture maps
Artifex	Mac, NT	Creating fire, smoke, water and other fluid things	Animators in need of collision detection particles

GETTING PLUGGED IN

Animators love features, but the sign of a truly good program is its ability to expand and grow without having to wait for future upgrades. Building a program with open architecture allows users to customize their software and vendors to update and improve their programs without major overhauls.

This is why programs that support plug-ins or extensions are so popular in the animation field. This capability is offered across the full spectrum of programs used in animation. Modeling programs such as Strata StudioPro offer extensions to expand its capabilities, and programs like 3D Studio Max and Electric Image support third party plug-ins that increase these program's already full feature sets.

For texture creation and image editing, few need to travel farther than Photoshop.

Without a doubt, one of the most over-used—but just so much darned fun—the Lens Flare filter is a simple way to dramatize a reflected light or a light source, as it was used here.

Dante, part of a plug-in collection by Northern Lights Productions, is a particle generation system that incorporates collision detection for realistic effects. Dante's effects simulate everything from smoke to water. Most animation programs now include particle systems as either built-in features or as add-on plug-ins.

Photoshop offers the ability to add plug-ins for everything from scanner drivers to a wonderful array of special effects filters.

On the editing end, programs like Premiere and After Effects support custom filters designed specifically for each program along with many of the same filters used in Photoshop, allowing the effects to be animated over time.

A great advantage of being able to tap into plug-ins is the reasonable cost. Many plug-ins are available as shareware or freeware. In some instances, these features can be limited, but if they handle a task that you need at the moment, they can be invaluable. If your software supports plug-ins, look at the software company's Web site. Most likely a library of plug-ins or a listing of what is available for that product can be found.

Photoshop plug-ins like Paint Alchemy, Eye Candy, and Kai's Power Tools can be invaluable aids in keeping the creative moment flowing. In the production environment, plug-in sets like Final Effects or Boris Effects give the special effects that can add magic.

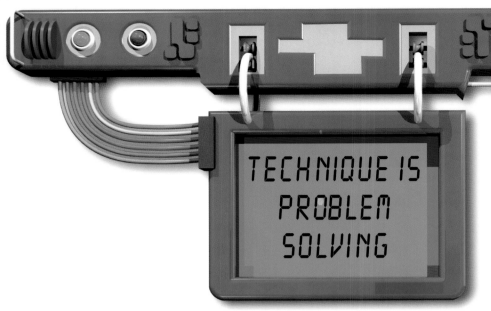

CHAPTER THREE

TECHNIQUE IS PROBLEM SOLVING

This section is filled with dozens of tips and tricks with a smattering of common sense—and hopefully luminescent inspiration. The key to working with the ideas discussed in the preceding pages is to tailor the concept to your software and your own style of working. Few tips could be lifted exactly and applied directly to your project, but they will form a foundation on how to achieve some interesting effects.

The trick to coming up with tips is simple: it is all based on problem solving. If your sink is clogged up, you may not realize it but you follow what is basically the scientific process. You pour water in and you realize its clogged. You know you have a problem and you get out the snake (or hire a plumber, whatever it takes) and clear the drain. Then you pour water in to check your results. You have identified a problem, worked up a solution, taken action, and checked your results. If it is still clogged, you do the whole thing again. Sometimes the problems facing an animator are not as complicated as getting the program to work or the hardware to function. The problem may be that motion looks stiff, trees look unrealistic, or renders are taking too long. This is when conceptual problem solving comes in.

The first step is knowing you have a situation that needs improving. While it may not be as obvious as having your sink overflow onto your new carpet, usually you can look at a work in progress and realize you need something. For our example, we have an animation of an engine block. All the parts are there, the animation is working fine, but it is lacking something. It is just too darned smooth, precise, and stiff.

The second step is coming up with a solu-

tion. For example, if you could expose the internal workings of an engine while it is still running, you would see frenzied activity and an almost blur of motion on the pistons, crank shaft, and valves. You have drawn all the internal parts exactly, yet this motion is not really present with your animation. If you speed up the animation, you lose key elements you are illustrating. You need a trick—something that fakes visual retention. You want to avoid motion blurs because you need crisp parts. The solution is to copy the animation file and run it 10 frames behind the original, but at a slight transparency. This leaves a light trailing ghost image and adds to the motion of the scene without muddling things up. This is the basis of the solution.

The third step is applying the solution. After playing around you decide a 15 percent transparency of the original five frames behind the original is the best deal.

Finally, you run the animation and see how it looks. If you need to, you repeat the whole process again.

This is how almost all of the tricks in this book were established: problem solving while creating animations and images for real-world clients with real-world problems. Some of them are based on common sense and some are explanations of how to do something so you do not have to figure it out from scratch, like creating GIF animations. Some are just neat little ideas that add a little drama and impact to animations.

Some, but not many, of the tricks are based on software products. Most of the tips and tricks work with any animation package on any platform, including SGI. While suggesting a specific software package may be a cop-out for a solution, in a few cases it is invaluable. You can struggle to come up with a realistic way to make trees, or you can go out and buy Tree Professional. Sometimes, it is best just to bite the bullet and buy the program.

Try not to limit yourself to the steps listed in the following sections. Branch off and add your own ideas and experiment with elements that are unique to your own situation. In some ways the tricks listed here are meant to act as a springboard for your own tip, trick, and technique development.

Good luck, and have fun.

CREATIVE PROBLEM SOLVING

All the tips and tricks in this book came from applying a loose version of the scientific method to come up with solutions to visual problems. Step 6 is all important.

1

Identify the problem. While this usually is not hard when dealing with technical problems, on the artist side it may be a little more ethereal.

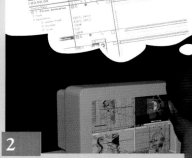

2

Think up a solution and outline the tasks needed to accomplish it. Consider your whole toolbox in the process.

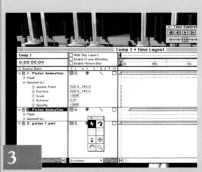

3

Apply the solution. More often than not, this means experimenting with all the variables.

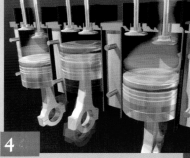

4

Check the results. Rendering out as small QuickTime or AVI files gives you good feedback.

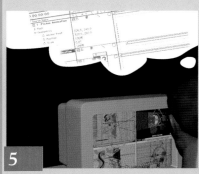

5

Things seldom work just right the first time. Build from your experience and start the solution process again.

6

Positive reinforcement is vital once you have reached your goal. Go to the fridge and get yourself a treat.

CAMERA FLY-THROUGHS

Fun to create, camera and object fly-throughs are one of the more dramatic uses of computer animation.

Often the camera in a scene is disassociated with the rest of the models and simply acts as the device the computer uses as a reference point for rendering the scene. In fly-throughs, however, the camera takes on a new role as an object. The camera's motions no longer just influence how the scene looks, but also how objects move within the scene.

To create a fly-through scene, objects are actually linked to the camera, so, when the camera moves, the objects move also. Since the objects are linked freely (as opposed to being locked), they still have their own motion. But linked objects' motions are always in reference to the main motion the camera is making, hence moving in the same direction as the camera.

In the cell example, an environment is built for the camera to fly through. A hollow tube is created using procedural colors (marble with reds and oranges to give it an organic vessel feel). Then the event marks that take the camera the distance through the tube, twisting and turning as it goes, are established.

Blood cells are created ("Blood cells" model is on the CD-ROM.) and linked to the camera with free (or unlocked) links. This makes the camera the parent object. Since the tube is dark, lights also are attached to the camera and the lights and camera fly along with the cells, following the motion of the "parent" camera.

Before the scene is rendered, the blood cells move, in relation with the camera, to various places throughout the animation. It is best not to make these motions at the same point or event mark as the camera. This allows smooth motion and keeps jerking to a minimum. The same technique could be used by attaching a camera to an airplane or spacecraft.

The blood cells above are pivoting and rolling in relation to the camera, but are linked to the camera's position.

Bouncing, rolling and flowing, the blood cells in this animation are actually following the camera's motions.

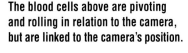

SETTING UP A FLY-THROUGH

Fly-throughs add drama to any scene. Creating them is a simple matter of assigning paths and setting up objects, lights, and the camera to interact with each other.

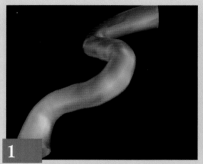

1 Create the model you are going to fly through. The model could be a mountain terrain or, as in this case, a hollow tube colored like a vein.

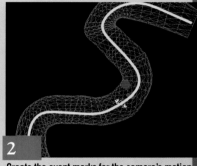

2 Create the event marks for the camera's motion. In this example, the camera flew through the vein, twisting and turning as it went.

3 Build the model that is going to do the flying, such as an airplane or blood cells, as in this example.

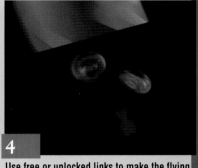

4 Use free or unlocked links to make the flying model (cells here) a child (linked) to the camera (parent).

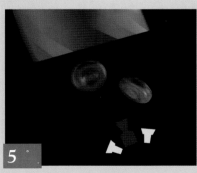

5 If your camera and your object of focus are moving, lights may need to move with them. Link the lights to the camera.

6 Move the objects (cells in this case) in relation to the camera at various points. Render the animation.

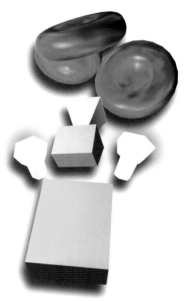

Another take on the fly-through concept is to create a new shape that becomes the animated element. The camera and lights are attached to the object so they can have more fluid motion without influencing the other objects (cells in this case.) The object is flown through the scene allowing for easy editing of the camera's motions as it moves through the scene. The camera can pivot on its own axis without swinging the lights with it. (In this case, the camera can weave and bob without the cells weaving and bobbing.) The base object should be made transparent to avoid showing up and also to eliminate any unwanted shadows.

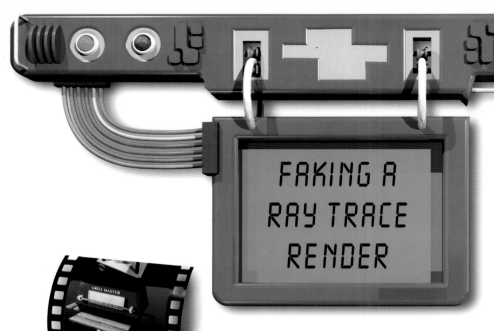

FAKING A RAY TRACE RENDER

Rendering out two animations and compositing them together may save valuable time. Consider doing the second, detail render (in this case, the glass on the grill) in a lower quality Gouraud shading if possible, saving even more time. If you are going to make the latter transparent, you may not need higher quality Phong shade. Increasing the oversampling or anti-alias setting may improve edge quality and make the transition between the composites smoother.

A time comes in every animator's life when a tight deadline makes a long render impractical. Looking at your creation, you realize it would render out quickly, but it needs to be ray traced to take advantage of transparency maps. Ray tracing is costly and more than doubles rendering time. Using a Phong render would kill the transparency, but would render in time.

A solution is to fake a ray trace by rendering the transparent objects separately. This technique saves time with complex renders if the transparency needs are modest—like the windows of a car or building. The price paid for this shortcut is fancy retractions (bending of light), but sometimes this is acceptable.

To use this technique, build a model keeping in mind your future plans. First some logic. If looking through an object, say a wall, you cannot throw a glass plate on it and plan to make it transparent. You have to "poke" a hole in the wall. In most cases, if you were planning to ray trace, this will be done already.

After your model is complete, select the object to be transparent and make it invisible. Render the scene. (An option to render invisible objects should be toggled off.)

Open the scene file again and make the trans-

parent object visible. Make **everything** in the rest of the scene invisible. If you saved all the event marks and key frames, the animation should place the object in the same exact position as the original render. Now, render this scene. You will be using this to edit on the final animation later, so render with an alpha channel for clean compositing.

Now take both renders and merge them together in your editing program. Place the transparent object on top. Change the opacity of the top layer to make it resemble the transparency of the type of material it represents. Glass usually looks good at about 40 percent to 70 percent transparent. (While the images are separate, experiment with changing the opaque item's hue or brightness to enhance the transparency effect.)

If objects in the model are in front of the transparent object (like the handle on the grill), you may have to render them separately as well. Whether you save rendering time or not is going to vary with each scene, but often the transparency can be faked in the editing process without having to use incredible rendering power.

GRILL MASTER

CREATING A FAUX RAY TRACE

Animators create false transparencies for two reasons. One is to save rendering time. The other is the control that working in multiple layers affords the animator.

1 Set up the model. Remember, you will be separating the elements for two different renders. Save different versions BEFORE editing.

2 Delete or make invisible the object that is supposed to become transparent. If you cannot make it invisible, delete the object.

3 Render the image using an alpha channel. The alpha channel is key to editing the images together later.

4 Delete or make invisible the object that is to stay solid. Use the same key frame or event mark information from Step 1.

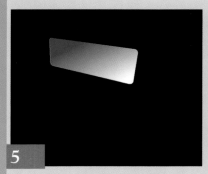

5 Render the animation again. This time, all you should see is the object that is supposed to be transparent.

6 In an editing program, bring the parts together. Put the faux-transparent layer on top and lower its opacity setting.

You may need to break the composite up in segments so that the layering still works. In this case, when the grill opened up, the window needed to disappear for a few frames before reappearing on the underside of the grill top again. You can do this simply by using "in" and "out" points in the editing composition.

MAKING 3D STILL ART FOR THE WEB

Everyone wants bold, interesting images for their Web pages, and while the rest of the world is struggling with Photoshop to make images look dimensional, you have already got all the tools in hand to do the job. Using your 3D programs to create Web art puts you into a visual class of your own.

Almost all modeling programs allow the user to output single-frame image files that can be edited for the Web. Most even support the creation of an alpha channel that can

The masthead for the Web page below was designed using 3D tools. The use of 3D art elements gives the designer a distinctive, colorful and dramatic alternative to traditional 2D art.

come in handy down the road if you have a GIF export tool such as PhotoGIF, which allows you to use the alpha channel information as a transparency map mask. If you do not have access to a program that lets you tap into the alpha channel for masking, there is an easy way around it.

Simply choose a background color that is not represented anywhere in your image. Render the final scene with the background color. In Photoshop, use the GIF export filter to choose the background color to be your transparency map. Be mindful of the background color selection. A neon yellow background leaves the residue of a yellow halo on a dark Web site background. Try to approximate the general color and intensity for your background color. Another route is to render with an alpha channel. Use the inverse selection of that channel to fill the area around your image. The same concerns about a background color apply here as well.

Image requirements for the World Wide Web are identical to conditions for creating animations for CD-ROMs and almost the same for video. All three media use low-resolution, 72dpi images and, with the exception of video, use the same gamma settings.

A big advantage to working with the Web is its flexibility. If you do not like something about a design element, you change it. Unlike video, print or CD-ROMs, once an image is done, it is done. The Web flexibility allows the artist to post an image, see how it works with the overall page then work with it until it is perfected.

Another advantage is the ease in cleaning up and improving low-resolution, single images in photo-editing programs like Photoshop.

Two formats exist for Web images, GIF and JPEG. GIF images allow you to take advantage of two important features in Web design: transparency maps and interlacing. Transparency maps allow an artist to silhouette images onto the background of the page. Interlacing allows an image to slowly build on a screen so that the viewer has something to view sooner. While download time is the same, interlacing can help break the tedium of waiting for an image to appear.

Now, back to page design. To avoid the standard rectangle- or square-shaped images, give the page some depth by fooling the eye. In

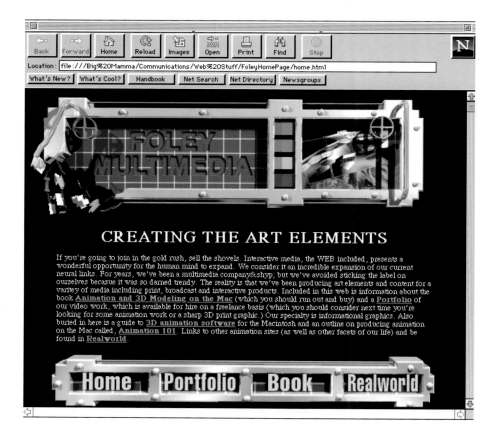

APPLY TRANSPARENCY MAPS

Two reasons exist for creating a fake transparency. One is to save rendering time. The other is the control that working in multiple layers affords the animator.

1 If the software does not support channels, render the image on a solid color similar to the image background. If it does support alpha channels, render with a straight alpha channel.

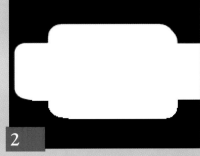

2 Open the image in Photoshop. If it did not render with an alpha channel, use the path tool to draw an outline (slightly inside the image) and save the selection. This creates an alpha channel.

3 With an alpha channel created use a plug-in program like PhotoGIF to save the image as a GIF using the alpha channel as transparency map information.

GIF or JPEG, design the Web page on a solid color and build your art elements on that same color. You may be able to get the color information from your page editor, but it may be easier to get the color by simply taking a snapshot of the screen. When you design the art for the page, use irregular shapes and even soft drop shadows that blend into the background color– giving the page a more dimensional feel. The final art can then be imported seamlessly into your page, since both have the same background color.

A drawback of the GIF format is that the image must be in 8-bit color (256 colors). While this lower resolution file may download quicker, some banding may occur. (Banding occurs when smooth gradations are broken down into coarser steps because of the limited palette.)

On the other hand, JPEG images can be saved in full, 24-bit color (millions of colors). This normally would create larger file-size images, but the compression used by JPEG creates tighter file sizes. JPEG files download quickly and look good, but there are pitfalls. All graphical browsers support GIF format, but not all support JPEG–although the most popular ones do. JPEG images cannot support transparency maps or interlaced images.

If you have worked hard on an image, you want it to look its best, and you want viewers to download the image, JPEG is the way to go. If you are concerned strictly with Web page design, then GIF has the most options.

When creating 3D elements for the Web, keep your audience in mind. Graphics generated on a Mac tend to be darker on a Windows machine. This can cause loss of detail in dark and shadow areas. When you post your images on the Web, you never know what type of machine it is going to run on. Keep it light.

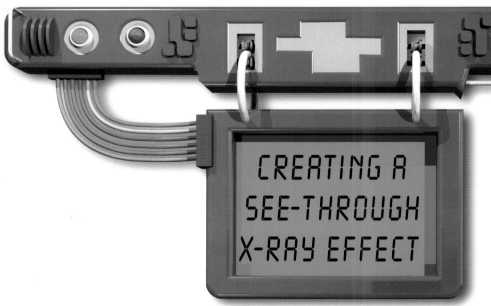

CREATING A SEE-THROUGH X-RAY EFFECT

Every so often you come across a technique that really brings out the power of 3D imaging. Considering that a lot of effort goes into recreating the existing world, or reasonable facsimiles there of, it is nice to come up with a trick that would be almost impossible to do in any other media.

One of those tricks is creating an X-ray effect, allowing the user to see into an object.

The still image below shows how the X-ray effect can be used. The scene required three layers: the craft's outer shell; the main, inner skeleton; and the equipment details. Each required a separate model and render.

One way of achieving this is to use a transparency map with a feathered edge. This technique has visual problems, not to mention the additional rendering time.

Another way to achieve this x-ray effect is in a post-production environment. You can futz with the results without having to render the whole project over again. This effect can be achieved on multiple layers. However, for this example we will focus on a simple single-layered transparency.

To build this composition, two renders are required. First we will focus on creating an X-ray effect for a still scene. In the next section, we will see how to use the same technique over time.

Since we are dealing with a still image, we can work in a program like Photoshop. Photoshop offers a perfect environment for creating X-ray effects. The key tools to use in the program are the layers and the erase tool.

To begin, set up the main object render. In our example, we used an image of the Hubble Space Telescope. The object and camera positions of the first, main render, will determine the position of the second render.

Figure out your final image dimensions and adjust your camera window appropriately. Keep in mind what you want to be showing on the inside of your object. In the Hubble example, we want to highlight instruments in the rear of the telescope, so we chose a rear perspective.

The craft is swiveled slightly so that when we do start working on the innards of the craft, we will be able to see what we want. The beauty of working in 3D is that at a later time we can adjust our angles and render again. Keep this in mind when you are setting up your render. A good idea is to place your object in the center of the world with a 0° X-, Y- and Z-orientation and adjust the positioning of the image in the window by moving the camera. This way when you start working on the innards, finding your orientation will be easy.

A departure from this method is to reverse the way you are working. Instead of stacking up the respective layers, it is possible and, perhaps in some circumstance desirable, to do just the opposite and cut holes into the object.

Instead of using a feathered eraser tool to whittle down the edges of an object that will lay on top, you cut a hole in the object with the

feathered eraser tool that will act as a window. The next art element is placed beneath the layer and becomes visible through the newly erased hole. One advantage of this is it allows you to create an artificial interior. If you placed an element in this second layer that had been rendered with an alpha channel and has void spaces, for instance, then a third layer can be placed behind it, colored, and even airbrushed to give the feel of an interior cavity.

The result is a believable space that mimics volume, with consecutive layers going deeper as you look into the object.

SETTING UP THE X-RAY EFFECT

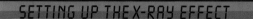

Half the work of creating an X-ray effect is done in carefully setting up the models. The other half is done in compositing the images, which can be done in Photoshop using layering tools.

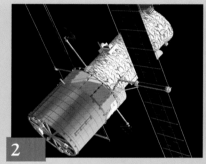

1 Start by building the base model and setting the camera position in the exact location for the final render viewed. Write down the coordinates of the camera– just in case.

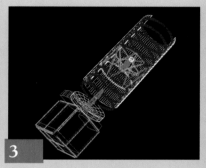

2 Render the base image for the model. Use an alpha channel to enable use of the alpha channel information later when selecting the final composite.

3 Set up the inside model that is to be seen as the x-rayed layer. Position it exactly so the base layer and the inside layer line up. Make sure the camera is in the exact position.

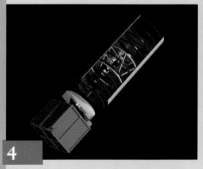

4 Render the model of the inside parts with an alpha channel. The alpha channel allows precise shape selection needed for tight cutaways when placing the image.

5 In Photoshop, create a new layer and open the base render. Select the image by using the "Load Selection" command and paste it in the new layer. Create another layer and do the same with the inside render image.

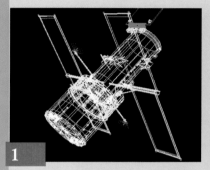

6 Using the erase tool set with an airbrush setting and the opacity set between 20-50 percent, begin to erase the edges. In this scene, you can see the top side has been erased, but the bottom has yet to be edited.

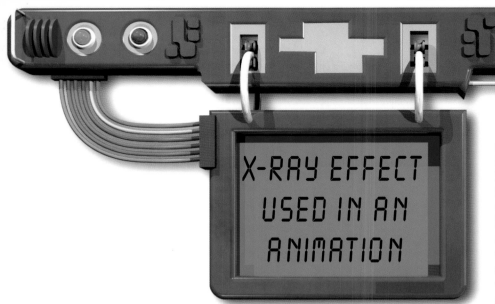

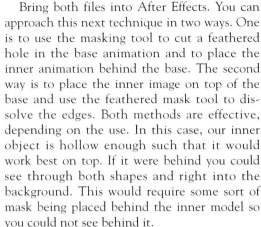

X-RAY EFFECT USED IN AN ANIMATION

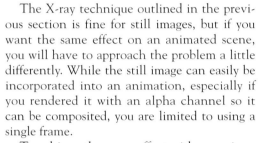

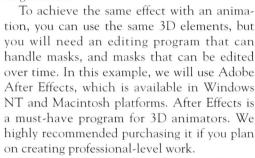

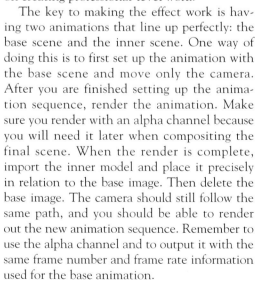

The X-ray technique outlined in the previous section is fine for still images, but if you want the same effect on an animated scene, you will have to approach the problem a little differently. While the still image can easily be incorporated into an animation, especially if you rendered it with an alpha channel so it can be composited, you are limited to using a single frame.

To achieve the same effect with an animation, you can use the same 3D elements, but you will need an editing program that can handle masks, and masks that can be edited over time. In this example, we will use Adobe After Effects, which is available in Windows NT and Macintosh platforms. After Effects is a must-have program for 3D animators. We highly recommended purchasing it if you plan on creating professional-level work.

The key to making the effect work is having two animations that line up perfectly: the base scene and the inner scene. One way of doing this is to first set up the animation with the base scene and move only the camera. After you are finished setting up the animation sequence, render the animation. Make sure you render with an alpha channel because you will need it later when compositing the final scene. When the render is complete, import the inner model and place it precisely in relation to the base image. Then delete the base image. The camera should still follow the same path, and you should be able to render out the new animation sequence. Remember to use the alpha channel and to output it with the same frame number and frame rate information used for the base animation.

Bring both files into After Effects. You can approach this next technique in two ways. One is to use the masking tool to cut a feathered hole in the base animation and to place the inner animation behind the base. The second way is to place the inner image on top of the base and use the feathered mask tool to dissolve the edges. Both methods are effective, depending on the use. In this case, our inner object is hollow enough such that it would work best on top. If it were behind you could see through both shapes and right into the background. This would require some sort of mask being placed behind the inner model so you could not see behind it.

The mask shape will have to be edited over time. Using a feather mask aids in the X-ray effect and is very forgiving in the editing of the mask shape over time. Feather settings of 5-15 pixels usually do the job. Shift the mask handles as needed as the animation progresses. The final result is an animated X-ray effect.

Since you are working in time, you can enforce the effect's reality by blending on the transparent layer over time. This technique works if the transparent layer is placed on top of the main layer. This way the opening of your animation can show the complete object, and then as time passes, you can blend on the new layer.

If your project requires the feathered hole approach, you can still achieve the effect, but it will be a little more complicated. Create a duplicate layer of the main layer and place it on top of the original. Use the feathered mask to poke a hole in the original. At this point, place the internal innards layer under the main layer. Over time you can now blend off the duplicate layer on top, revealing the main layer with the internal portion revealed below.

No matter which route you go, it is best to leave the transparent layer slightly opaque. This increases the X-ray effect. In the first method this means making the innards layer slightly transparent, say around 80 to 90 percent. In the second method this means leaving the duplicate layer present above the other layers and making the transparency around 10 to 20 percent.

SETTING UP THE ANIMATED X-RAY

The key to setting up the animation is working in a program that supports feathered masks that can be animated, such as After Effects, which is available in both Windows NT and Mac platforms.

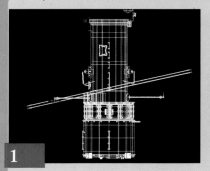

1

Set up base animation. Move camera and keep base object still. Render animation with an alpha channel. Remember frame settings.

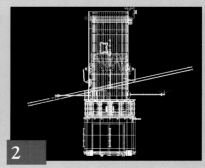

2

Import the interior model and place. Delete the base object. The camera still should have all the original settings.

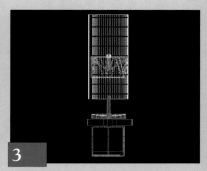

3

Render new scene using the same camera. Input all the same frame settings (size, duration, frame rate) and use an alpha channel.

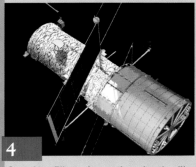

4

Open After Effects. Import the animation file. Animations rendered with an alpha channel can be composited on a background later.

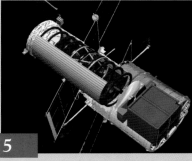

5

Import interior animation file at exact starting point as base animation. The alpha channel will silhouette the image onto the base.

6

In the layer window, draw a mask for the interior slightly inside the image. The feather works on both sides of the line.

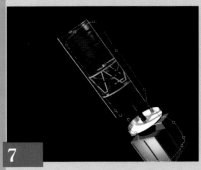

7

Move the time cursor down a few frames and re-adjust the mask so it lines up with the area you want to show. Continue to do this for the entire animation.

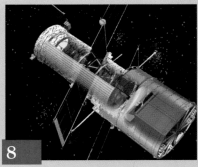

8

The results are an X-ray image moving in time. Changing overall opacity of the interior layer to 90-95 percent gives a see-through look.

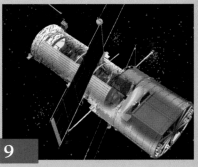

9

For overlapping parts (like solar panels), import the base animation again and use the masking tool (no feather) on just the portion to patch.

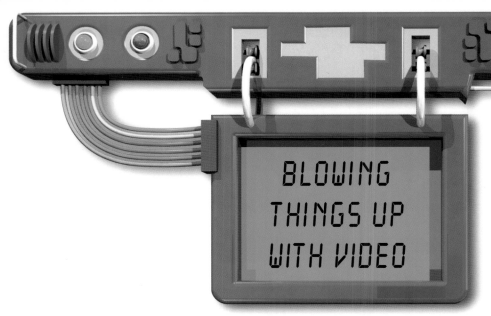

BLOWING
THINGS UP
WITH VIDEO

As much as we might try to suppress any violent tendencies, there is nothing quite as much fun as blowing things up in 3D animation. The urge probably has some grounding in the omnipresent feeling animators get over the worlds they create, possibly harking back to the Greek gods who, after making the immortals, had endless fun messing with their lives.

You can take three routes for blowing things up: importing explosion video, generating particle effects and creating a truly nasty lens flare. In this section we will cover importing video.

Most people are not industrious enough to film their own explosions, but help is at hand. A company called Pyromania supplies CD-ROMs with digitized explosions for both the Windows and Macintosh platforms. Artbeats also sells a selection of digitized explosions. The CD-ROMs contain a collection of impossible-to-model effects, such as explosions, flames and smoke. The process is not automatic. The users are left to figure out how to bring the digitized frames into their computers.

Two formats are supplied: single, full screen (640 x 480) PICT frames, each individually captured for the highest quality; and smaller QuickTime movies. While importing the QuickTime movies is the easiest route to go, the quality of the output and the limited size make importing the PICT frames a better choice, even for smaller files.

Programs like After Effects and Premiere can import the PICT file sequences. Most of the effects do not come with alpha channels, which is fine. Creating the smooth, realistic edges of a flame would be too hard with an alpha channel. The trick to introducing the fire or smoke imports is to use the "lightest" or "luminance" layer effect.

With Premiere, place the explosion track in the "S1 layer." Select the file, and under the "Clip" menu, you will see "Transparency" as an option. Select it. Then, under the "Key Type" option, choose "Luminance."

In After Effects, import the file and select the file in the construction window. Under the "Layer" menu, select "Mode" and use the lightest effect.

With both programs, you can tweak the layer's contrast and brightness to achieve better effects. Since you are using the lightest ink effects, you will want to make sure that your background image is darker than the explosion itself. For this reason, an explosion at night is going to be a lot more impressive than an explosion during the day.

Explosions out of the can may not always give you the effect you want. Some customization is usually required. For example, explosions are seldom where you want them on the screen, the length you need them to be, or the right size. The tools available in programs like After Effects and Premiere come to the rescue and allow you to get just the effect you need.

The first thing you might want to do is to create multiple layers of explosions. In After Effects you simply place the explosion from the clip window as many times as needed. In Premiere you create as many additional tracks as you need. If working with a single explosion file, you can position the starting point of each explosion farther down the time line, effectively extending the duration of the explosion as it builds upon itself. By shifting the position of the additional files, you can eventually fill a screen with an explosion that initially filled only a quarter of the screen.

Since explosions are pretty dynamic, the color shifts that happen when the explosions overlap each other give the explosion enough variation so that the repetition is not too obvious. Keep in mind that explosions usually have a short shelf life. If you are filling up a screen with small explosions, you will have to make sure you have some filler explosions to cover the gaps created when more mature fireballs dissolve and new ones are being born.

If possible, use this technique to combine a series of different types of explosions to add

CREATING A VIDEO EXPLOSION

An important factor in setting up the animation is working in a program that supports feathered masks that can be animated, such as After Effects, which is available in both Windows NT and Mac platforms.

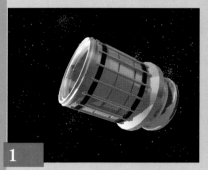

1 Import base animation, rendering and compositing in the editing program. This enables explosion placements in front of and behind the base.

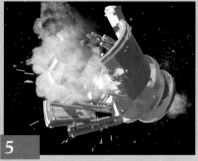

2 Import the explosion file. If using Pyromania's explosions, the best results can be obtained by importing a PICT sequence.

3 Select the layer and use either the Premiere transparency feature or After Effects lighten feature. Tweaking contrast and brightness helps.

4 Position and scale the explosion file as needed. In some case you may want to start with the explosion at 10% of its original size and expand over time up to 150%.

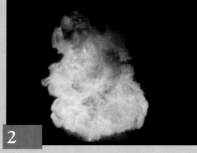

5 Use the same techniques outlined to introduce other elements like sparks (above) or smoke. Secondary elements add realism and drama.

6 When the explosion is over, blend off the final frames to make the transition believable.

impact to the scene. For example, combine the explosion with a shower of sparks. The sparks–using the same lightness method–are brighter than the main explosion, so they boldly jump out from the rest of the scene.

If you still want a longer explosion, or if the explosion is too fast, you can always do a time stretch on the file to change its duration.

You also can scale the explosions to start from a small pinpoint to one filling the screen. Explosions tend to be transparent and ethereal in nature, making them forgiving if you want to enlarge them past their 100 percent size. This is something you would never do with a solid 3D object. In some cases, the explosions still hold up even when enlarged as much as 150 percent.

Of course nothing adds more realism to an explosion than a good BOOM in the animation's sound track.

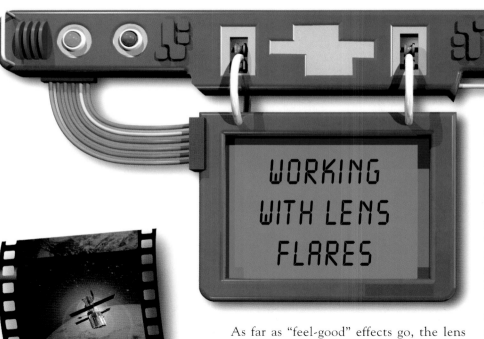

WORKING WITH LENS FLARES

The scenes below demonstrate the impact a simple lens flare has on the entire scene. While a hotspot is created at the flare center, lens reflections influence almost every pixel of the image.

As far as "feel-good" effects go, the lens flare is on top of the heap. Lens flares look good, are easy to apply, and do not add excessively to render times. The key to lens flares is restraint—do not use them too much.

Most modeling programs offer support for applying a lens flare to animations. However, you may be better off waiting to apply the effect in the editing process. The reason is simple. If you do not like the effect, you do not have to render the whole animation again to readjust it. While you can render out single frames to get a feel for how the lens flare is working, the effect can take on a life of its own. Unusual things can happen, like the lens glare creeping in and leaving undesirable effects throughout the entire animation.

A reason for rendering a lens flare in the initial animation output is that the flare has a realistic effect as it plays over different objects in the model. This also can be achieved with editing, but the key is how you set up your ani-

mation in the first place, and then how you edit the file. Since you work in layers during the editing process, you can apply the lens flare to just the layers you want, or composite the scene and apply the effect to the whole production.

You can use lens flares for several purposes, including simulating bright objects (such as the sun, muzzle blasts or reflection hotspots), faking explosions, or creating—simply enough—the effect of light hitting the viewing lens (ergo, lens flare).

In our example, we use a lens flare to fake a reflection on the side of a satellite as the bright metallic object peaks over the horizon. While the reflection in our example is severe to demonstrate the point, the effect in an animation is to immediately direct the viewer's attention to the spot where the satellite will come into view. A flash one quarter of the size we used would be effective in this task.

The use of the lens flare is as vital as any other part of the animation: the stars, the earth, and even the satellite. The use of the device should be considered as carefully as the other elements, and this includes overkill. You might be tempted to have a few flares just for kicks, but hold off if you can. A single, well placed flare can be effective, yet a series can be unsettling and annoying.

The satellite example has three main layers: the star background, the earth and the satellite. The intention is to hit the flare to simulate the satellite breaking over the horizon as it flies towards us. Initially the satellite will be non-existent, but as the flare fades off, the satellite will become larger. To keep from blasting the first frames of the satellite away, apply the lens flare to only the stars and earth. Before you apply the effect, make sure all the elements are in their final position. In this case the earth and stars will move slightly as the satellite appears and moves forward.

In After Effects, you build the entire project and select the layers you want to pre-compose so you can apply the lens flare to the new composited layer (in this case the stars and earth). The satellite layer would be unaffected by the flare.

In Premiere, set up the stars and earth first. Apply the lens flare, then compile ("Make Movie" command) the animation at full resolution. The output is imported into a new Premiere movie and the satellite is brought in

CREATING A FLARE HOTSPOT

Lens flares are supported by all the major modeling and editing programs. Editing the flare after the render allows the user flexibility of making changes and fine tuning without having to re-render.

1 Import your elements in layers. Merge or pre-compose layers where you want the flare effects. In this case, the stars and the earth were merged.

2 Position the flare. Start its intensity off at the lowest setting. If the object is sweeping across the screen, change the flare position to match.

3 Increase flare brightness over time. Flares tend to be short-lived– keep duration about one second. After peaking, reduce brightness until it disappears.

on the "Superimpose" track using the "Alpha Channel" option in the transparency settings.

In applying the filter, you will want to move the center point of the flare over time so it lines up in the proper hotspot. Change the intensity of the flare by bringing it up from a small dot to a bright flare and then back to a small dot again. In this example, the flare only needs to last about one second from start to finish.

You can apply a lens flare to a scene and have it affect other elements as well, giving it realistic impact on the scene, as in a reflection. There are a couple of ways to do this and both involve working with layers–making a program that allows working in layers and masks, like After Effects, indispensible.

The process involves duplicating the layer that you want to affect. A good example would be looking out the window of a building, where you want to have a lens flare from a reflective surface in the distance, but you also want it to affect the window as well. The last thing you want, however, is a lens flare on the inside of the window frame or the wall. To prevent the interior lens flare, you create a

duplicate of the layer and use the masking tool to draw the mask for the glass portion of the window. Now you can apply the filter to the new layer. Since you might not want the effect as strong as the original lens flare, you might opt for using a lighter flare or run the duplicate layer slightly transparent.

One great thing about After Effects is that you can copy the attributes of a filter. So if you have your flare moving and changing intensity, you can copy these settings and paste them into the attributes on your duplicate layer, giving the feel of change-over-time for both the original and the reflected duplicate.

Lens flares are fun, but sometimes you do not need that hotspot and would rather just have the lens reflection effect, as in the case of a panning camera. You can remove the hotspot by moving the center point of the flare off the viewing area and using a wide lens setting for the flare. This will add to the reflected effect by the lens.

Keep in mind that there can be too much of a good thing, so keep the flares to a minimum. More than one for any scene can be annoying.

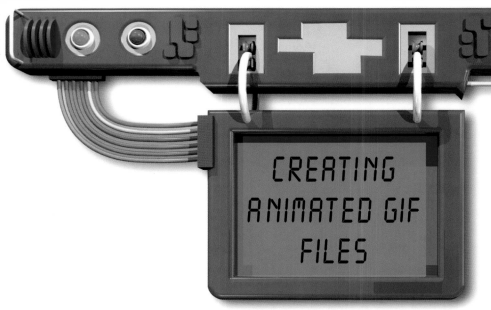

CREATING ANIMATED GIF FILES

3D elements add life to Web pages. In some cases, such as the logo below, a straight-forward 2D illustration takes on a new life. This logo was imported into a 3D program from Adobe Illustrator. Once it is in the 3D world, it can have the added benefit of being animated.

A straightforward way of getting animation into Web sites is to use animated GIF files. The GIF format was developed years ago for CompuServe users to share image files. While the single-frame GIF file is a de facto standard on the Web, the format also supports multiple-block files, meaning it can contain more than one image per file. These images are stacked on top of each other and played back at interval settings (fast or slow) determined by the author.

The two main steps for producing animated GIF files are creating the animation file and editing the output file into something the Web can swallow. Since this is a book on 3D animation, we assume an interest in out-putting 3D animation files. You can achieve many interesting effects working in just 2D editing programs such as Premiere, After Effects, or Director. The animated 2D output follows the same path as working with 3D files. However, the initial creation takes a different approach.

First some video and broadcast reminders. If you have been working with animations for video, remember your output is now for computer screens and will not be as bright as working in NTSC video standards. The same is true for CD-ROM animation output. As for platform differences, Macintosh monitors are lighter than the VGA monitors in the Windows/DOS world. This is key since you do not know who will be viewing your final product so try to work on the light side.

Broadcast animations run at 30 frames per second (FPS). CD-ROMs clock in around 15 FPS. And in the Internet world, the rate at which each frame is held is user-defined. The default for most GIF editing programs is one-tenth of a second, or 10 frames a second. So when you are creating your animation, determine how much download agony your viewers will have to experience. The law of the land is to keep it small and short.

Animated GIF files stream when download-ing—meaning part of the image is put on the screen and the rest of the image flows behind it as quickly as the modem speed can handle it. For small files, you might be able to have a simple file play for a very long time without delaying the viewer. With larger animations viewers will experience some lag time. What can you do to stream effectively? Use small, 2-bit animations with 1k per frame is the best approach. Obviously this kills big, bright, flashy animations. You can have the flash as long as your audience is very patient.

A simple animation may have 10 frames. In our example, we rotated a logo. Spinning logos seem to be popular for two reasons. First, in mid-rotation, not much of an image area exists, mean-ing a quicker download. The second is the spin loops back into itself, so the file can be set to loop and the logo can spin until the viewer gets dizzy.

The Global Net logo (at left) is an extruded shape, rotated on the X-axis with the lens set at 28mm to add some depth. A monotone theme allows "sampling-down" the animation to a tighter palette, making the file even smaller.

SETTING UP THE ANIMATION

Spinning logos may not be the best of use of GIF animations, but they do serve a decorative purpose and are easy to set up. Use a copy of the first event mark to end the animation, therefore making a continuous loop.

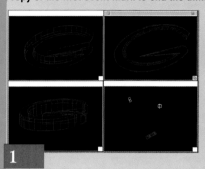

1 Create the logo of choice. In this case, a simple logo outline was imported from Adobe Illustrator into an animation program.

2 The object is spun over time. For a complete 360°-rotation, make sure it is going in the right direction by using three 120°-rotations.

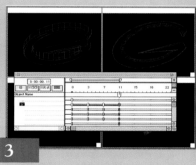

3 To insure the loop is complete and the motion returns to the start, copy the first event mark and make it the last event mark.

4 Keep the number of frames to a minimum. Ten frames of a very small frame animation may be acceptable.

5 Render the animation with an alpha channel. Unless importing the output directly into a GIF creation program, the alpha channel is needed for editing.

6 The final output can be rendered in 24-bit color and dithered down in either the editing program (preferred) or the GIF creation program (often with less control).

The animation takes place over 10 frames. Set the frame count to 11, since the 11th frame will be the same as the first after the logo has spun all the way around. Delete the extra frame in the editing process or before exporting the final GIF file.

After your animation is set up, your choice of formats for rendering depends largely on the 3D program being used and the GIF creation software used to work with the file. Take the output animation directly from the 3D animation program and into the GIF creation program. But reasons exist for taking the animation into an editing program first. You have more control over transparency maps and gamma settings if you output your animation to be edited first. In the editing program, you can adjust changes like color, so the best route to go will be to output your master animation from your 3D animation program with an alpha channel.

All editing programs for Windows and Mac (i.e., Premiere, After Effects) allow users to

tweak the animation and output in a format that the GIF creation software can handle. In your editing program, either select a background color or create a tone that will be used as a transparency map. While you are in the editing program, experiment with filters and effects. More importantly, scale the file to the exact size you want the final GIF to be and you can manipulate the gamma settings and color balance to get the exact look you want. If you rendered an object with dark shadows or objects, this is where you could raise the levels to adjust for lighter output.

When you are done editing, output the animation in a file format compatible with your GIF creation program. GIF Construction Set for Windows takes AVI files and Video for Windows. GIF Builder for the Mac takes sequential PICTS, PICS, or QuickTime. Both shareware programs give users all the control they need to convert productions to animated GIF files.

When importing files, you have a handful of options from which to pick. They include delay time, transparency, disposal method, loop, palette, and depth.

Delay time: This option establishes the amount of time you want a frame to hold stationary. The settings are based on 100th of a second, so for a relatively smooth animation you might choose 10, which displays 10 frames per second. For more of a slide show, you might increase the number to 100 to give each frame a one-second display.

Animated GIFs can be as simple as spinning logos or as complex as anything you see in the movies (perhaps not quite as large). In the example below, the animated GIF used in the lower right of the page represents a large, if not unwieldy, use of GIF animations at 20 frames, 8-bit and 160x120 pixels. This 90k file would take over a minute for a Web surfer to download using a 14.4 modem.

Transparency: With transparency you can drop the background out of your animation by choosing a color to be transparent. Be careful not to use a color that is in your animation, or it will go transparent as well as the background. This is a good reason to use an editing program between the 3D animation program and the GIF editing program. If you are having dropout problems, go back to your editing file and tweak the color balance or the overall levels of the animation layer without affecting the background layer. By doing this you can work around the dropout problem without having to re-render the animation.

Disposal: Without the disposal method in an animation with a transparency, you can see the previously stacked up GIF files behind each subsequent frame. To avoid this you can set the disposal method to restore the background. After each frame is played the background is restored, so the files do not build up on each other.

Loop: You can set an animation to loop over and over again, which can be distracting, or you can set an animation to play a set number of times. Some GIF creation programs allow for the animation to repeat after a certain time period.

Palette: While there are a few different schools of thought on palettes, there is no single correct choice between using your system palette, creating a palette, or loading a palette. The choice depends on your audience. If all site viewers were Mac users, you could use the system palette with no regret. If all viewers were Windows users, you could use the Windows palette with fine results on all Windows-based machines. If a color in your animation is in the viewer's palette, it will look fine; if it is not, the color will be dithered with existing palette colors to approximate it.

The end results depend on your image. Some images might look okay on both Windows and Mac, while some may not. The closest thing to a compromise is to use the Netscape Navigator palette, which is based on the Windows palette. This works fine with most browsers and since the Mac handles color better than Windows, there will not be much degradation on that platform. A customized Netscape palette is available on the CD-ROM or from http://www.foleymedia/tips/gif.html, the authors' Web site.

EDITING THE ANIMATION

Bringing your animation output into an editing program gives you a good deal of control over elements such as background colors, compositing and effects.

1

Bring the animation file into your editing program and adjust the window size to fit your composition. In this case, the logo was brought into After Effects.

2

Editing may involve compositing elements. Here we created a drop shadow using a black, solid object with an oval, feathered mask with 50 percent opacity.

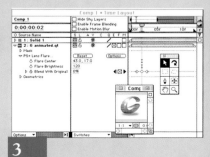

3

Take advantage of effects tools. We placed a lens flare over three frames as the "G" begins its rotation.

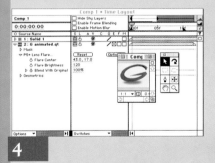

4

One of the more important edits made in an animation is the background color. You can change your background to match your page or make a solid tone that later will be used as a transparency map.

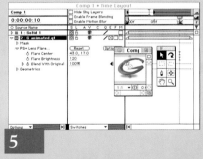

5

If the last frame is the same as the first in the completion of the rotation, remove this last frame by moving your outpoint up a frame—making for a smooth loop.

6

Output the animation in a format your GIF creation software will import and dither down the export to 256 colors.

Depth: Experiment with lower color depth settings. Since 8-bit is as high as a GIF goes, if using a monotone image, you may be able to reduce the depth to 4-bits. This helps with download time. When building your animation, also keep in mind that blends between like colors (dark blue to light blue) will be more successfully dithered than blends across a rainbow of colors.

When making adjustments to your animation using the above settings, make sure all the frames are selected in the frames window. If you

have only a single frame selected and you set up your transparencies, timing and depths, you will notice nothing happens except perhaps a little flash while the animation is playing. That flash is the single frame you adjusted. So select all the frames and then make the adjustments in bulk.

After making the adjustments, output your file. The file can be treated just like a single-frame GIF file. Write your HTML tags in just the same manner as a regular GIF file, or import the animated GIF file into an HTML editing program just like a normal GIF file.

The current versions of Netscape and Internet Explorer support animated GIFs. Some older browsers may not.

You have the same image constraints when you create animated GIF files as you do when you create single files, except for some of the little quirks that pop up when working on still image–these stand up and scream at you when they are animated. The biggest concern is dithering. Since all images in the GIF format must be reduced to 256 colors, some amount of dithering usually takes place. Since 3D art elements look great because they are so photorealistic, they are also the ones that suffer the most. Those fine shades of colors in shadows and highlights almost always break down when filtered through that pesky 256 color barrier. A dithered still image may have an annoying grainy texture to it, but with an animated element, those little grains can come to life and add undesirable noise to your animation.

There is no sure fire way around this, but you can do things to help alleviate the problem. Simply enough, restrict your palette as much as possible.

If you need to produce a 3D animation GIF file but you do not have the time or the inspiration, you can animate a static 3D element in an animation program and simulate the motion. An example here is an element like a compass rose that you want to spin on a page. Render out a frame of the object straight on and import the final product into your animation editing program. Then rotate the single element 360° over time and export the file like you would if it were a standard animation file. One thing about this method is that the image uses the same palette; therefore, it is possible to reduce the object's pixel depth without getting any annoying pixel flickering, and give yourself an animation that downloads faster. The same concept can be used for one or more elements that need to change positions during the animation. Working in layers, you can play several static files off each other, rotating and shifting, and then output them as a single animation file.

In the Web world, make a habit out of making everything as small, tight and quick as possible. While this may kill some creativity, in other ways it creates a challenge for animators to work in a demanding medium. It is easy to come up with a great looking animation in full screen full color, but it is a challenge to impress people with a 40 pixel x 40 pixel, 4-bit animation that is 15 frames long!

THE QUICKTIME OPTION

And then there is QuickTime. Much like the contrast between GIF files and JPEG files, you might increase your image quality with QuickTime, but you pay the price in a couple different areas. Your QuickTime movie will have to live in its little rectangle, since QuickTime cannot support transparency maps, and not everyone will be able to see your creation. Viewers will need to set up browsers to use MoviePlayer or another QuickTime viewer to allow for the playback of movies, while animated GIF file support is built into all the popular browsers.

One huge bonus for the QuickTime option is sound support. Animations come to life with some kind of audio track, and QuickTime is the best way of achieving this on the Web.

Creating QuickTime movies for the Web is pretty straightforward. Most editing programs animators use for both Windows and Mac have support for QuickTime output. If your software does not support QuickTime, utility programs are available for file conversion, such as turning an AVI file into a QuickTime movie.

Animated GIFs are not limited to spinning logos or even moving objects. Flashing, blinking, glowing buttons, and border elements can add life to a Web page. While this book focuses on 3D animation, you can use many of the same tools, such as After Effects and Premiere, to create some sparkling effects with 2D tools and filters. All the rules, from transparency maps to interlacing, apply the same way they would with a 3D animation. One of the many examples of creative GIF usage, shown below, can be found on Eric's Homepage, http://www.geocities.com/ SiliconValley/9974/

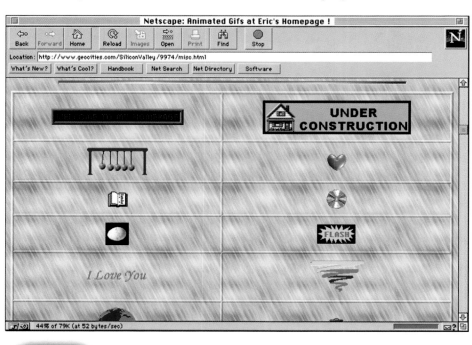

MAKING THE FINAL OUTPUT

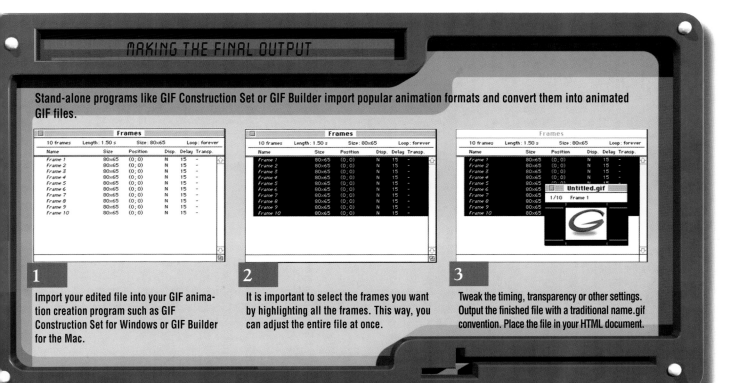

Stand-alone programs like GIF Construction Set or GIF Builder import popular animation formats and convert them into animated GIF files.

1 Import your edited file into your GIF animation creation program such as GIF Construction Set for Windows or GIF Builder for the Mac.

2 It is important to select the frames you want by highlighting all the frames. This way, you can adjust the entire file at once.

3 Tweak the timing, transparency or other settings. Output the finished file with a traditional name.gif convention. Place the file in your HTML document.

When creating an animation production, you will want to start off with the highest quality source files. If possible, do not compress any of the original animation files you are creating for import into your editing program. If you do, the files will be double-compressed when you output them for your final movie and the results will suffer.

QuickTime movies tend to be large, and compression brings down the image quality. Programs such as Movie Cleaner Pro help out by allowing for tighter compression and cleaner output than most exports created directly from editing programs.

To compress images, QuickTime uses an assortment of CODEC (compression-decompression) from which the user can choose. At this writing, there is not a specific CODEC written for Web use, but a few options are available. Most animations work well with the Cinepak CODEC, which is very lossy, but makes small files. With the quality setting put to high, the format creates pretty solid animations. Keep in mind that QuickTime movies

include sound, and that soundtrack can sometimes be as large as half the movie's size. You might want to sample the audio down to 8-bit before creating your final QuickTime output. When you create your file you will want to flatten the image and make it self-contained so other users can run the document. If your authoring program does not support these features, you can open up a movie in MoviePlayer and do a "Save As" which is where these options will present themselves. If you want your movie to be viewed by multiple platforms, you will have to flatten it.

If you are working in Windows, you can put an AVI (Video for Windows) file on the Web, but users in other platforms will have to have special software to convert the files after downloading them into their hard drives. With QuickTime, most browsers support the format and allow an animation file to be integrated into the page layout, unlike earlier days when the file needed to be downloaded and played back in a separate window.

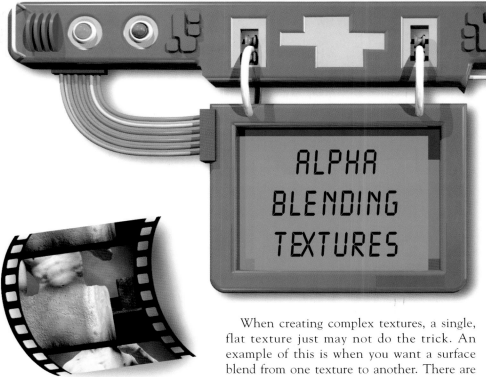

ALPHA BLENDING TEXTURES

When creating complex textures, a single, flat texture just may not do the trick. An example of this is when you want a surface blend from one texture to another. There are two ways to approach this. One is to create the texture merge in your image editing program and map the results on the model. While this solution may work most of the time, you might want to alter an existing map without creating an entirely new map. The second method involves blending the new texture on top of the old texture using the modeling program's alpha reveal features.

Almost all programs support some kind of alpha reveal feature. The programs require a texture map that has the texture's color on the RGB level and an alpha channel with the masking information. Areas in white will be shown on the final textures and areas in black will not be seen. Grey values will give shades of transparency.

In our examples (below and next page), we are using a dark boulder texture throughout the entire scene. The same texture that is applied to the surface and other monoliths is the same exact texture applied on our dominant monolith, only on the dominant monolith we have added a new texture layer.

To create this effect, create an underlying texture (the boulder texture shown here). In this example, we have created a bump map on the boulder. This gives a bumpy realism to the object. To do this, we copied the surface into the alpha channel and increased the contrast to make the bump more severe. Some programs might require the bump map to be imported as a separate document.

We then created the blending surface. Here we used a marble texture from the Wraptures collection. An alpha channel and an uneven gradation are created. To make the transition, Photoshop's lasso tool is used with the feather set on 50 pixels. The top selection is drawn and then filled with white. The white layer will be the area that shows through.

Then textures are applied. The boulder texture is applied first and its alpha channel is used as a bump map. Then the marble texture is applied on top, using its alpha channel for the reveal.

Both use a cubicle map. The boulder texture tiled on both X- and Y-planes, but the marble tiled only on the X-plane so it does not repeat vertically.

This technique can be used for a wide variety of effects. Surfaces in the real world are seldom pristine and flawless. Merging two textures into each other allows the animator to create surfaces that reflect real-world textures. The alpha reveal does not always have to be a gradation. It can simply be a slightly undulat-

APPLYING ALPHA-BLEND TEXTURE

Almost all modeling and animation programs support multiple layers and alpha blending or alpha revealing. To edit the texture, use any image editing program that supports alpha channels, such as Photoshop.

1 Create the underlying texture. Above, boulder texture from the Wraptures CD was selected. This surface will be the first texture applied.

2 To make the surface rough and realistic, include a bump map. To create a bump map, copy the texture, place it in the alpha channel and tweak the contrast.

3 Create the texture you want to blend. In our example, we want to go from a rough stone to a smooth marble.

4 Create an alpha channel for the new texture and create a blend from black to white. If the texture is going to tile, make sure the left- and right-hand sides match up.

5 Apply the first texture. In this example, a cubicle map was used with an intense bump map and a slightly higher specular highlight.

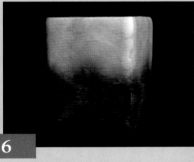

6 Apply the second texture and adjust the texture dialog settings to use the alpha channel as a mask. Indicate that the alpha channel will be used to reveal.

ing grey scale, allowing the underlying map to fade in and out of the main texture color, achieving the variations found in most objects. A few examples might include carpet stains, fading wallpaper and the whitewash look on bricks that sit under siding.

While you would not want the whitewash stain on a brick wall to be present in the actual surface tile of the brick, you would want it on the top of the wall where the brick meets the siding. To accomplish this, create a light white, slightly noisy surface. The alpha channel would be a drippy but soft texture that runs partway down the wall. The final result would be a texture that would run only slightly opaque so that the surface of the brick would never be covered completely, but would give the appearance of a stain running down the wall.

USING KPT'S SEAMLESS WELDER

The three earth layers were developed from photographs of the different rock strata. To make the raw source work as a tiled texture, KPT's Seamless Welder was used.

Every so often you come across a tool and you want to run out in the street and shout, "This is so cool." Most of Kai's Power Tools fall into this category. While your neighbors may not understand your delirium, most animators appreciate the features the set of Photoshop filters provide. Available for both the Windows and Macintosh platforms, the plug-in filters just sit and wait for you until you need them.

Sometimes you never use a filter, but on that occasion when you need a specific effect and the filter provides a path for getting there, you will be glad you made the investment.

For 3D modelers and animators, the most relevant and useful filter in the pack is the Seamless Welder. The Seamless Welder's only function in life is to create seamless, tiled textures. Previously, creating tiled textures meant using the offset function and patching over the seam or using the feather tool to duplicate and flop sides. Seamless Welder quickly and cleanly does away with this housekeeping chore in a very straightforward manner.

To use the tool, you first need your texture. In our example, a geologist mailed in a 3"x5" photograph of a geological cross-section. The photograph was scanned in, but needed to be tiled so it could be used on the model. With the scan open in Photoshop, the "selection tool" was used to select an area just over 10 pixels square inside each edge. The Welder works by using the information on the outside of the selection area to blend in the opposite side. So creating the selection is key if the filter is to work properly.

With the selection made, choose "Seamless Welder" from the KPT filter selection under "Filter." Your options are simple. The most important choice is whether you will create the tile by using the seamless method or the reflection method. The seamless method uses the 10 pixel area for copying the information exactly as it is, over to the other side. The reflection method uses a mirror effect. Experiment with each setting. Textures with strong direction, such as wood grain, will not work well with reflection. Other surfaces, such as carpet or grass, seem to work fine.

Once the choices are made, click on the green "do it" dot. The document remaining **is not** a finished product. Before doing anything, copy the selected object and create a new document (it should come in at the size of the copied area) and paste. The new document is your seamless texture.

Along with the Seamless Welder filter, two other tools are of interest to animators. The Texture Explorer creates a seemingly infinite range of textures. While many of the textures right out of the can may not serve much more than visual clutter, with a little time and

EDITING THE SEAMLESS TILE

KPT's filters run on Photoshop's Windows and Macintosh versions. For modelers and animators, the Seamless Welder filter is an invaluable tool and worth the cost of the entire filter package.

1 Create your texture. In this case, a 3"x5" photograph from a geologist was scanned. Avoid glaring marks or hotspots that will be noticeable when repeated.

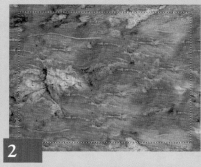

2 Select the area for tiling. Seamless Welder needs 10 pixels of information outside the selection area to make the transition between sides.

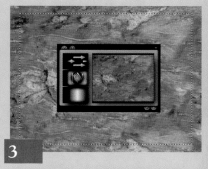

3 Choose "Seamless Welder" tool from your filter menu. Experiment with the options by clicking and dragging. The defaults are usually what you will need.

4 Your options include a seamless weld (left) which blends the two opposite sides or the reflection (right) which mirrors the same side. In different cases, each provides different results. So experiment and try each.

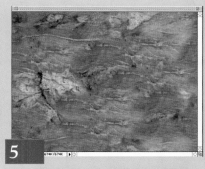

5 After the filter has run, the selected area is what you want. Create a new document in Photoshop and paste the new selection. Save in a format acceptable to your modeling program.

6 Apply the final texture to the surface of your model. The same technique used for the surface color can be used for creating bump maps.

tweaking you can create textures for everything ranging from wood grains to animal skins.

The second fun tool is the Planar Tile tool. The results of this tool are the same as taking a texture and applying it on an infinite surface and rendering it– without ever leaving Photoshop. There are occasions when animators need a simple planar background on which to animate their element. The Planar Tile tool does the job quickly without any hassle. You will most likely want to use the Seamless Welder on the file first, so the image that is created tiles cleanly. One solid use for this is creating an atmosphere. You can use the on-board Cloud filter to create a cloud screen, then use the Seamless Welder followed by the Planar Tile and vertically flop the results.

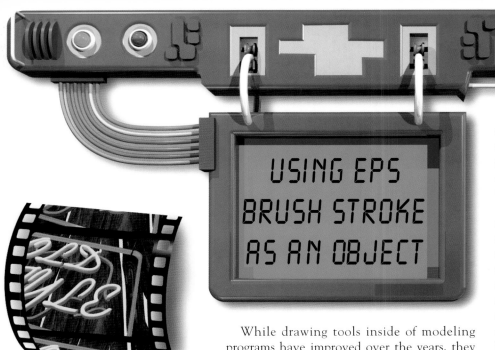

USING EPS BRUSH STROKE AS AN OBJECT

The sign below was created entirely in Adobe Illustrator using the brush stroke tool and exported as an EPS document. The resulting file was imported into a 3D modeling program as an extruded shape where it was textured, lighted and rendered. The wood planks also were created in Illustrator and imported as extruded objects.

While drawing tools inside of modeling programs have improved over the years, they still often fall short of the many features available in dedicated 2D drawing programs. This does not mean that the tools are not available for the animator; it just requires an occasional stroll outside of the modeling program to tap into some of the strength available in other programs. Macromedia Freehand and Adobe Illustrator are available in both Windows and Macintosh platforms. Shapes created in these programs can often be imported into modeling programs as extruded shapes, directly or with the help of optional plug-ins.

The brush tool, one of the tools found in Freehand and Illustrator but not in modelers,

allows a single brush stroke to create a shape and then has the results available as an EPS path. The brush tool gives the animator a quick way to make flowing, yet solid shapes with easily edited girth.

In our example, we created a neon light with the aid of Illustrator's brush tool. The text and the underlying connectors for the sign are drawn in two groups. First, the text is drawn using the brush tool set at seven pixels and rounded end-caps. Once drawn, the file is saved as an EPS document and all the text elements are grouped together. For the second group, the connecting elements are drawn with the tool brush set at five pixels, simulating the blacked-out neon tube that connects the letters together. Then the text elements are deleted and the resulting file, with only the connectors, is saved as an EPS document.

The results are two files, one for the text, the other for the connectors. Both files are brought into a modeling program that accepts EPS outlines (in this case Infini-D), positioned and textured appropriately. A round bevel is applied to the objects to give them a glass tube effect. You can produce varied results by playing with the settings available with the brush tool, such as line endings or calligraphic effects.

This technique touches on the whole concept of using outside drawing programs to create objects to import into 3D programs. In many cases 2D drawing tools provide a solid, reliable way to create complex shapes. Illustrator and Freehand offer a wide variety of drawing and editing tools that are a boon to shape creation. Drawing tools, in comparison to 3D tools, usually do not require too much RAM, so you can run both the 2D program and the 3D program at the same time and quickly flip between the two.

Drawing programs offer features, such as calligraphic pens, that can create free flowing art elements, adding a natural, non-mechanical touch to 3D models. Since the origin of many 3D drawing tools is in the CAD world, all too often the final results of 3D modeling look like they were drawn on a computer. Reaching out into more natural programs allows the animator to avoid this.

Even when direct import options are not available, animators might want to consider drawing with illustration software or traditionally by hand and using template import features or

USING EPS BRUSH STROKE FOR 3D

Illustrator and Freehand offer flexible brush tools that create closed EPS paths. These paths can be imported into many modeling programs and be extruded to create 3D shapes.

1 Set variables on the brush as needed. For the neon light connectors shape, we used a five-point brush stroke with rounded-end caps.

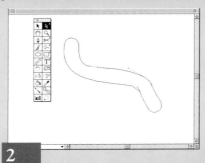

2 In wireframe mode, you can see brush stroke handles. If you want, tweak the shape before exporting it. When done, save the file as an EPS document.

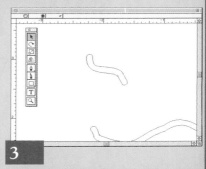

3 Bring in the EPS file. Some programs, like Electric Image, have plug-ins to allow the proper import of EPS shapes.

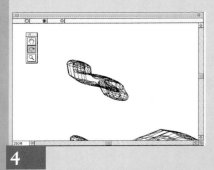

4 For our neon light, we applied a bevel to the entire shape to give it rounded edges. Place the object in the scene where it belongs.

5 Apply textures as needed. With the neon light, we put a nice yellow glow on the bright parts and turned off the object's ability to cast shadows (a light would not cast shadows).

6 Render the finished scene. Save the original EPS file. If you do not like the shape, you can go back and adjust it.

a scanner to bring in template elements before relying on the computer to generate all the art. Often a subtle curve or a gentle form is lost when it is perceived as a portion of a pre-existing primitive or fashioned with the basic drawing tools found in most modeling programs.

Working with a 2D program may simply form the foundation of a more complex shape that can evolve further once imported into a modeling program. Most modeling programs allow for outlines to be imported from other programs for editing. With this technique, you can create a template for building facades or automobile parts. The template can be imported and then improved upon given the range of tools available in the modeling program.

SETTING MOOD WITH NATURAL LIGHT

The role of visual elements is to tell a story or set a scene. We have been looking at the world since day one and our brains have come to expect certain things from our surroundings. If you do not supply the details, like long soft shadows in a sunset scene, then a little warning bell goes off in the viewer's mind. If you do it right, nobody notices– and that is a good thing.

Wildly photorealistic scenes are not just hatched. Every nook, cranny, texture and essence needs to be captured. While the nooks and crannies fall into the modeling realm and the textures fall into the mapping world, the essence remains the ethereal element that can make or break a scene. Creating natural lighting is key to lighting both indoor and outdoor scenes. The difference between lighting and natural lighting is that you illuminate objects in your scene with lighting. Natural lighting follows the principles and guidelines of a real setting.

In outdoor settings, the sun establishes the standards for the way light is used in a scene. The variables are many, but common sense is your best guide. In our examples, we show a scene at noon and then at sunset. At noon, the light is high and harsh with harsh shadows. At sunset, the light is low and dimmer with soft shadows. A tint of color appears in the sunset light, as if it were slightly orange. With the exception of a single light change, the whole mood of the image is altered.

In creating this scene, a parallel light source was used. This creates a good overall light source for outdoors, without the hotspots found with a radial or spot light. For the noon light, the source was not directly overhead. A slight offset helps catch more interesting edges and helps create shadows that otherwise might disappear with a light directly above.

To make life interesting, the sun not only keeps shifting in its position in the sky each day, but it keeps shifting around during seasons as well. Winter is a time of longer and softer shadows and warmer light. Summer is a time of harsh, direct, cold light.

Geographic location influences lighting as well. You could occupy several valuable hours calculating the exact arc of the sun for any given latitude for any given day. Suffice it to say that you should just keep these shifts in mind so your scene reflects them. In some instances, the wrong light setting kills the scene's realism.

If working on an animation or a sequence of events that play over the course of a day, consider the light's continuity as much as you would any other element in the production. For example, sunsets do not always mean a darker scene. Vertical elements can seem to glow at this time of day as they catch the sun's horizontal, multi-colored rays of light.

Since almost all of the lighting indoors is artificial, this lighting presents a whole new world of possibilities. Lamps have different temperatures and run at different colors, so it is a good idea to keep this in mind even if you are not modeling a lamp, but only placing a light source in the scene.

The lighting in an office scene, for instance, would have a fair amount of icky fluorescent green-yellow. While you would not want to make it as intense as what you might find in a photograph of an office, you would want it to be present. Regular light bulbs burn a little on

ADJUSTING LIGHTS AND MOOD

In the scenes below, the only element that changes is a single parallel light source. Alterations made in its location, shadows, color, and intensity change the mood of the entire scene.

In the noontime setting, the light is positioned above the scene with shadows adjusted at a low softness setting and a bright white light color.

For the sunset scene, the same setting is used but the light is lowered a few degrees above the horizon. An orange color is applied and the shadow detail is softened.

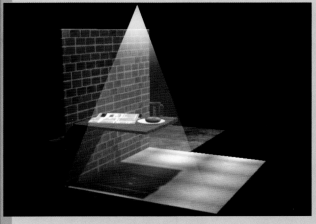

Placing a parallel light directly above the scene wipes out almost all of the shadow detail. By offsetting the light slightly, interesting things happen in the shortened shadows.

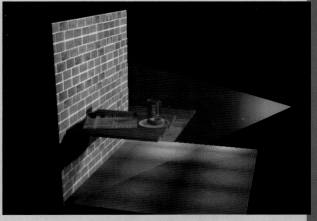

In the sunset image, the light source is brought above the horizon, creating long, soft shadows that our brains automatically associate with this time of the day.

the yellow side and halogen bulbs run between white to white with a little blue.

When creating a new light for a scene, do not just pop it into place and forget about it. Consider what is generating that light and think of it as just as important as any other element in the scene. Alter the settings for shadow softness, light color, light type and intensity. Otherwise the light may get lost in the shuffle and do more harm than good.

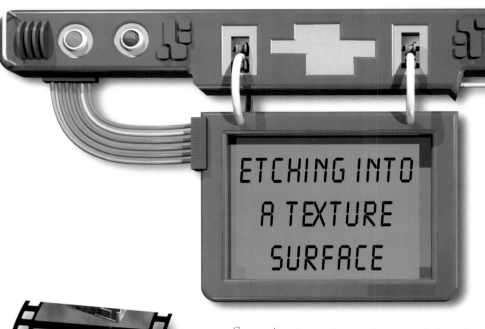

ETCHING INTO A TEXTURE SURFACE

Etching or branding can help add realistic detail to objects, such as the wooden crate below. The crate was modeled in form•Z and animated in Electric Image.

Sometimes you want a texture to go beneath the model's surface. Bump maps are the usual route animators take to get an etched or branded effect, but bump maps can only go so far before they start falling apart. Falling short of actually carving into the model with a boolean function, one quick way to achieve a realistic effect exists.

The etching effect described here requires three key elements: Photoshop, Alien Skin's Eye Candy, and a modeling/animation program that supports an alpha channel reveal.

Eye Candy makes short work of creating the image and should be considered part of any animator's toolbox of tricks. Eye Candy is available for both Windows and Macintosh.

Start by creating the color of the area that will be inside the etched area. In our example, we are branding wood, so we created a dark, grainy texture using the Noise and Emboss filters. If you were etching glass, you might make a frosty grain with the noise tool.

Next create an alpha channel that shows the area to be etched. Areas in white are the etched area. Go back to the RGB layer after the channel is created and load the selection. Apply the Eye Candy Carve filter. Adjust the settings until you have the best feel for the shape you want. Save the file when done, making sure the alpha channel is still included. The alpha channel will act as a mask on the final composite.

Now, create the base surface. This is the surface that the object will have before the etch is applied. It can be either a texture map or a simple colored surface, as in the case with a glass sheet.

In your modeling/animation program, apply the base texture map or surface color to the object. In our example, we used a wood texture to be applied to the wood slats in the crate model.

Now the fun part. Bring in your etch texture map with the alpha channel. Apply and position it on the surface of the object (on top of the base surface map), which in our case is the wood grain. Make sure the etch texture uses the alpha channel to reveal the etch texture, masking out all the other parts of the surface texture. Some programs do this automatically. Others require that the texture's attributes be adjusted for the alpha reveal.

To increase the etch effect, use the alpha channel as a bump map. Edit it as a separate document in Photoshop, reversing the colors so the black parts recede, and apply a slight blur so the bump map has a nice grey-scale edge to it, allowing the computer to create a better illusion of a bump.

Because of the interesting way Eye Candy's Carve tool works, it serves a host of other purposes for the animator. If you need an uneven surface for land or corroded metal, you can quickly create a bump map by using the Carve filter. Simply create a document in Photoshop and fill it with a neutral gray color. Using the "Lasso" or any other selection tool, create a series of selections reflecting the amount of variety you want the surface to have–lots of lit-

HOW TO MAKE AN ETCHED TEXTURE

It is easy to create an etched or branded texture using Photoshop, Alien Skin's Eye Candy and a modeling/animation program that supports alpha channel masking for textures. Both Photoshop and Eye Candy are available for Windows and Macintosh.

1 Create the texture to appear in the etched area. If you are etching frosted glass, you may want a grainy white. For our brand, we used a dark, grainy brown.

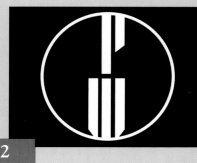

2 Make an alpha channel and create the image to be etched. Areas in white will be the final etched area.

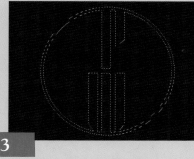

3 Go back to the main color and load the alpha channel selection.

4 With the area selected, use Eye Candy's Carve filter. The settings will need to be adjusted depending on the width and depth of the carve desired. Save the file with the alpha channel intact.

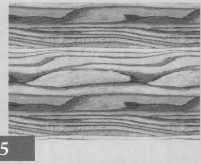

5 In your modeling/animation program, apply the base surface to your object. In this case, a tiled wood surface was applied first.

6 Next apply the etch surface using the alpha channel reveal. Since the area used to create the initial carve is white, the same area will appear.

tle selections for more coarse surfaces, and a handful of larger ones for a less detailed result. Apply the filter to the selection and play with the options using the "Preview" window to give you a feel for the final result. When you have found the combination you like, select the "OK" button. The result is a file perfect for bump mapping because the edges of the carve will be a nice smooth gradation and the internal parts of the carve are dark, or push in, when applied as a bump map. If you want the results to pop out instead of indenting in, simply inverse the selection in Photoshop. Using a bump map created in this way adds character to an otherwise flat surface.

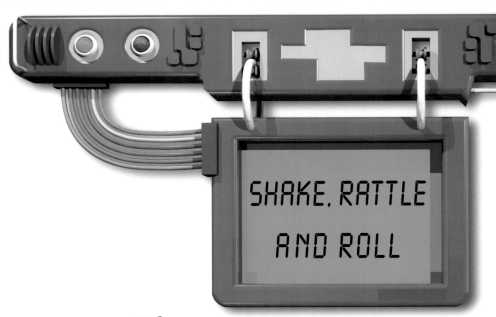

SHAKE, RATTLE AND ROLL

A straightforward animation of the engine below would not represent what we really see without some trick to fake visual retention. To accomplish this, a single layer was rendered in Strata StudioPro. The result was repeated in three layers in After Effects, offset slightly in time.

Most animation programs handle motion admirably, yet none address the kind of visual retention that we are used to in the real world. While motion blurs help accent an object's motion, sometimes this isn't enough. The result is a hard-edged motion that can sometimes seem unnatural, specifically with objects that are moving quickly.

If you rendered an animation and the result seems to be lacking the emphasis of the object moving over time and space, you may want to try the following post-production trick.

In your editing program, copy your animation layer and paste the copy directly on top of the original. Change the opacity of the copied layer to 30 percent. You will not see any difference because both tracks are playing at the

same time. Here is where the magic comes in. Shift the copied, slightly transparent layer slightly to the right so that the motion of the copied layer is slightly delayed. How far you slide the transparent layer depends on the amount of motion you want. Sliding too far results in an unbelievable, visually confusing image. What you want is an image where the copied layer is just barely trailing the original layer.

The next step is to bring this layer on shortly after the motion starts. If your animation starts with a static image and begins moving, you do not want it starting with the transparent offset– that would not make sense. Blend in the layer over time. One second is fine for most animations, depending on the speed of the object. Experimentation is the only way to get this right. If the motion slows and stops during the animation, you will want to blend off the transparent layer.

You can use a single transparent layer or, if it works for the animation, you can apply multiple offset transparent tracks. The latter can get noisy, so you may want to alter the transparency of different trailing layers to aid in the "reality" of the image. For example, the first trailing layer is set at 40 percent with the second trailing layer at 20 percent. The engine image (left), uses three layers: the original at 100 percent, the second at 40 percent and the third at 30 percent. Since the motion is repetitive, short and fast, this many layers works fine. However, the motion of a bullet–which is linear–would be accented best with just a single additional transparent offset layer.

If you want to get fancy, apply a motion blur to the second layer in the production program or re-render the animation with a motion blur if your modeling program supports motion blurs.

Experiment with changing the transparent layer's position slightly over time to accentuate the motion, with the offset getting further and more transparent as the object's speed increases.

If your original animation does not move enough to give the effect the impact you desire, you might want to increase the shifting effect by actually moving the duplicated layer, as well as shifting the layer over time. Most animation editing programs allow the user to change the position of an element, such as an imported animation file, over time. You will be able to shift the orientation as well, so when the original file is playing, the ghosted dupli-

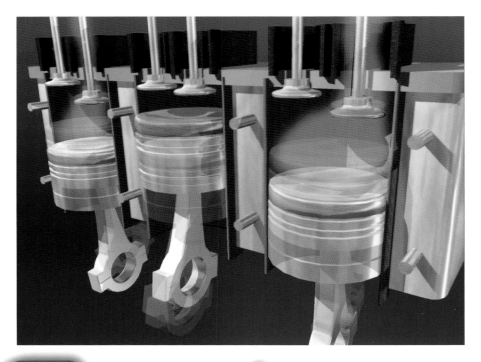

CREATING MOTION OFFSET EFFECT

You can apply an offset motion effect to any animation, regardless of what program you model it in. All you need is an editing program to create the offset, such as Premiere or After Effects.

1 Create the animation file. If your image does not run full screen, render with an alpha channel so you can bring in a background later.

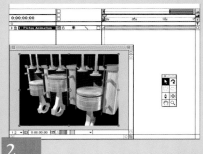

2 Import the animation file into your editing program. Most editing programs support transparency layers, which is key to creating the effect.

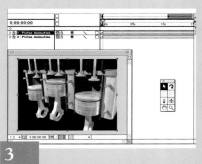

3 Duplicate or import the same animation file on top of your original. This will be the copy that you offset.

4 Slide the new layer to the right. This causes a slight delay in the time when these frames are played. How much you slide to the right depends on how quickly the object is moving across the screen. Adjust as needed.

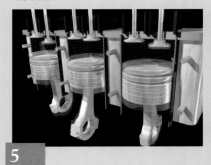

5 Make the layer slightly transparent—usually 20-40 percent will do. Since the layer is playing behind the solid original, there will be a ghosted effect. Blend the transparency on and off if the motion begins and ends in the scene.

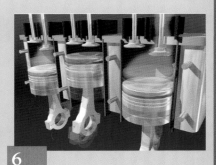

6 Use as many transparency layers as you like, but do not use too many and make it unnatural. Play with applying a motion blur to the transparent layer for added realism.

cate can shift in position as well as roll clockwise or counterclockwise to help accentuate the desired motion.

While this will most likely add to the finished animation's final render output time, the results will be worth it. Many motions that benefit from this effect are short-lived anyway and occur as the beginning or ending of a sequence, like the barrel of a gun jerking up when fired or a plane hitting the ground during a crash. Make sure you blend the offset files on and off so their existence is more natural and not too jarring.

Tricks like forcing visual retention into a scene add an unnatural element into an otherwise straightforward scene in hopes of making the result more believable. You must use good judgement in each case. Just because you went through the trouble of creating the effect does not mean it should be obvious.

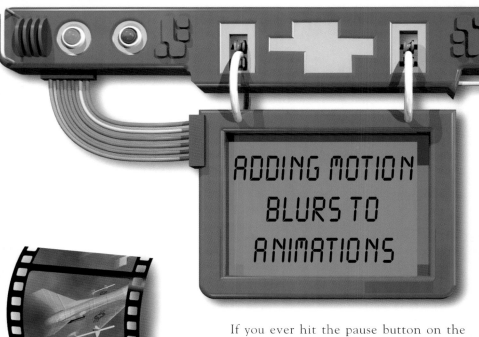

Working with an animation program that does not support motion blurs does not limit you in creating realistic animations. The blur can be applied in the editing process. The model (below) was rendered in Infini-D, brought into After Effects, and a copied layer was blurred with a feathered mask that affected only the trailing edges of the airplane.

If you ever hit the pause button on the VCR when an object (person, tennis ball, aircraft, whatever) is moving quickly across the screen, you will notice that even though the moment has been captured and the frame is still, motion is still very evident in the static frame. The motion is represented by a blur. Fast-moving sequences may seem clear and crisp, but in reality, they are blurry when you look at them one at a time.

To create realistic motion, this effect has to be mimicked. Unless you have created an animation of ice melting, chances are you will need some degree of motion blur to achieve a perfect animation.

Many programs support motion blurs that are applied during the final render. The good thing about internal motion blurs is that they are self-regulating. If an object is moving slowly, there may be no blur. If it moves quickly, there might be a large blur. The bad thing about these rendered blurs is that once you have rendered the blur, you cannot change it unless you re-render the animation. Motion blurs also add a considerable amount of time to the rendering process.

Whether you want to avoid the above pitfalls or you do not have a program that supports motion blurs, you still can achieve the effect by creating the motion blur in your editing program. All the popular editing programs have built-in blur functions or support plug-ins that create motion blurs.

How you approach the blur depends on the effect you want to create. Keep in mind when you are setting up your animation that your individual elements may take to a blur well, but you might not want to blur the whole scene. For instance, if you had an animation of a ball bouncing, you would want to render the scene of the room where the ball is bouncing separate from the ball. When you composite the images later, you can apply the motion blur to the ball, but the room will stay clean or crisp. If the camera is panning around the room, it can blur at a lesser setting than the blur on the ball. This attention to detail determines the realism of the animation.

When editing the animation, you may want to blur the whole object or just a portion of it (as in the jet's trailing wings).

To blur the whole object, simply apply the filter and alter the direction of the blend in the direction that the object is moving. Alter the distance of the blur to match the speed of the object moving on the screen. Do not be too tight with the blur. Objects close to the camera moving very fast can hold a blur of 20 or 40 pixels with no problem.

You also can apply blurs to portions of objects, as long as your editing program supports a masking feature. Copy the moving object into a new track so that it lies on top of the original animation. Use your mask tool with a feather tool to select the trailing ends of the object and animate the mask over time so that it stays with the object. Apply a blur to the copied layer and you will have a nice partial motion blur.

POST-PRODUCTION BLUR

If your modeling program does not support motion blurs or you did not have time to render out the effect, all is not lost. You can work in any editing program to apply a post-production motion blur.

1 Render out your animation without a motion blur. Images that work best are objects to be composited on a background after the render.

2 Apply a blur to the object. If altering the amount of the blur over time, make it a long blur with fast speeds and a short blur as the object slows down.

3 Composite the animation with the rest of the scene. Combining sharp still and blurred moving objects makes the scene realistic.

Because of the nature of the beast (blurry), motion blurs can be pretty forgiving. Try not to fixate on what an individual frame will look like. Play the animation back in realtime to get a feel before you begin tightening up the blur or altering mask positions. You will notice that, like in the real world, things happen fast and blur quite a bit. But taken as a whole, things hold together pretty well.

You might want to try a slight offset on a copied blurred layer as well. To do this you create duplicate layers of the original animation segment and place them slightly offset in time and position from the original to simulate the effect of visual retention. After the new layer (or layers) are created, apply motion blurs to each layer. Make sure you adjust the new layers to be mostly transparent so the effect is not too distracting. Additional motion blurs on multiple levels in varying degrees of transparency are bound to increase the time it takes for your editing program to render out each frame, so make sure it fits into

your schedule. It would not be unusual for a 30-second animation with no motion blur to take 10 minutes to render to disk. With a few additional motion blur levels, that rendering time can quickly grow to an hour or longer.

If you want to simulate the effect of a camera lens adjusting focus, or having foreground or background elements coming in or dropping out of focus, you can apply a Gaussian blur to different layers. If you are planning to do this, plan ahead so that you render out different elements of the animation as separate files so they can be imported into their own layers. If you have already rendered out your scene and the elements you want to work with are on the same layer, you might be able to use masking tools to select areas to bring in and out of focus.

While motion blurs work well with linear motion, some moves, like a camera rolling, might be better served with a quick application of a radial blur, which smudges the edges around a center point.

USING GLOW MAPS AS FAKE LIGHTS

Lights are a necessity to animators, but they also can be a luxury. Like most luxuries, too much of a good thing can be costly, and the price to the animator for excessive lights is rendering time. Each light used increases the calculations needed for each frame. It is easy to double your rendering time by adding a few additional lights.

One way to work around this is by using glow or luminance maps to simulate the existence of multiple lights. These maps will not shed any true light on the scene, but they can lend the impact of having a series of lights by faking the results of a lit surface.

All major modeling programs support some kind of glow mapping– the ability to take an image file and map it to a surface so that the selected region has a luminance. While the effect may look like a light is shining on the surface, the rendering time required is dramatically lower.

A single glow map may have several, if not dozens or even hundreds of areas that can brighten an object. A glow map with hundreds of small squares might be used to simulate the many windows on a skyscraper at night. A single round glow map might be used to make a single button glow.

While the edges of the squares for the sky scraper would be sharp, the simulated lit surface of an object would more likely have soft edges. The closer a light source is to an object, the sharper the edges, while the further a light source is from an object, the fuzzier the edges. Other ways to achieve soft edges is with a Gaussian blur on the glow area or a feather tool when creating the glow area.

A prime use of this indirect lighting is sconces. A row of sconces along a dark corridor provides a nice feel. But if each of those sconces had an individual light, the scene would take forever to render. Instead of using lights to cast a short beam onto the wall, a glow map can simulate the light above the sconce.

A panel (below left) is lit by a series of lamps without a single light source inside those lamps. The panel is lit by a soft glow map repeated under each lamp.

To create this effect, a five-inch square, new document is created in Photoshop. The main RGB image is left white and a new alpha channel is created. Inside the new alpha channel, the circle selection tool is used to choose a large circle in the middle with plenty of room on the sides. The selection is then feathered (in this case with a 15 pixel). The selection is made white by either deleting the area (with the background color selection set to white) or filling it white. The resulting file is saved as a PICT file with an alpha channel. The PICT file then is mapped onto the surface of the panel in Electric Image, using the alpha channel as a luminance map. The luminance level is adjusted to give a slight highlight to the area without being too bright. To complete the effect, you may place a sphere where the light bulb would be and adjust the object's luminance to resemble a real bulb.

The scene (below) was lit by only one light and a series of glow maps to simulate the lights from the multiple lamps. A backlight also was used to add impact to the scene.

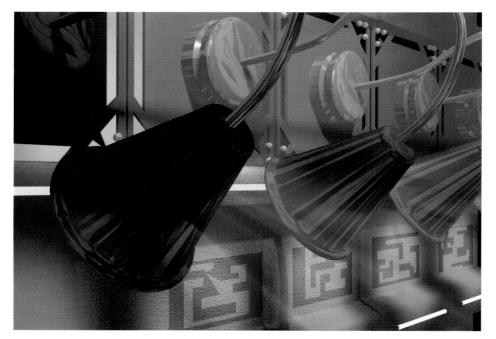

GLOW MAP EXAMPLES

All major modeling and animation programs on both Macintosh and Windows platforms support some kind of glow or luminance map. Here are some examples.

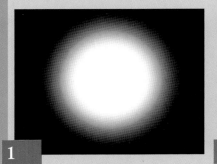

1

The glow map was created by making an alpha channel with a soft white center that serves as the luminance area.

2

Applied to the surface, the glow map looks like the surface area lightened by the bulb in the lamp, but there is no light source in the lamp.

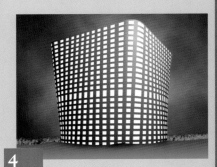

3

To create the windows, a series of rectangles are used. Depending on the program, either the light or dark areas become the glow area.

4

Mapped and tiled to the surface, a simple shape quickly becomes a building with all the lights on.

5

Like highlight maps, if you change the intensity of the glow map—as done here with varying shades of grey—you affect the final result of the map.

6

The varying shades in the glow map give the building a more realistic feel with the lights from each office shifting in brightness.

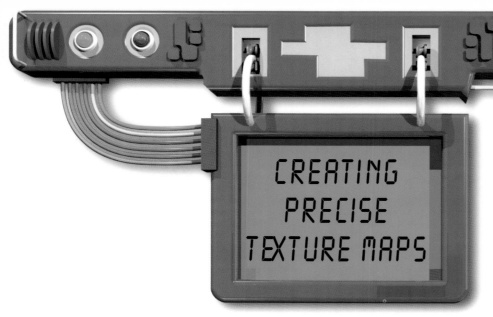

CREATING PRECISE TEXTURE MAPS

In some cases, the texture map dictates what the final shape of an object will become. But more often, the texture map is dictated by the shape of the object. Sometimes a texture map simply gives a general textured feel to a surface. In other cases you may have an extremely precise texture map that needs to go in an exact position on the model. In this case, you might need to coordinate carefully between your modeling program and your image editing program to get the desired results. If you were creating an airliner model, you would want to make sure the windows and the airline's logo are exactly positioned. If you are a little imprecise, the flaw will be obvious. While positioning the texture map is critical, the initial step of creating a texture map that lines up with your model is key.

The first step in designing a precise texture map (when the texture is to fit into an existing model) is to create a template of the model part (or parts) to which the texture will be applied. This is pretty simple. The Mac system allows for a "Command-Shift-3" to get a screen dump, and several shareware utilities can get you a Windows screen capture.

Position the model in the view in which the texture will be applied. In the example, the side of the land formation is what we will be creating a texture to fit. To get the template, a screen dump was made of the object's right side. Use an

To get the strata lines to follow the surface of the model, a land shape template was created and then used as a guide to create the texture map, which was then applied to the shape.

CREATING THE TEMPLATE

The first step in creating precise texture maps is a template on which to build. All programs and platforms allow capturing an orthographic image from the scene. The diagram (below) explains how to obtain the template.

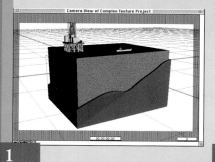

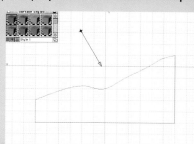

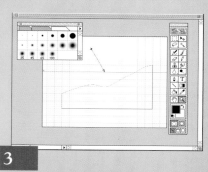

1 Build the model. If you are working with several textures, assemble the whole model and get as many templates as you need in one fell swoop.

2 Obtain a site view of the object by either saving the view, rendering out a still of that area or using a screen capture utility. Make sure your view is orthographic to avoid perspective distortion.

3 Import the template into your image editing program– one that supports multiple layers is best. In Photoshop, your template becomes the background layer by default.

orthographic view in the window you are capturing to prevent any perspective distortions.

If you do not want to mess with screen captures, simply render out the scene from the vantage point needed and use the rendered image as the template. If you go this route, remember to set the lens to an orthographic projection. If that is not available, set the lens to an extreme telephoto setting– this will help reduce perspective distortion.

Some programs with three-space (top, side, front) editing areas may allow you to simply save the current window as an image file. Since you should be working in orthographic mode in a three-space setup, you will get an automatic template.

After you acquire your template, you will want to open it in an image editing program that supports layers. Photoshop is perfect for this. The background layer will be your template, building textures on top.

Before you experiment, scale the image to the size you will want your final file to be.

This may pixelate the template if you get much larger, but it does not matter because it is used for position only. Do not scale up **after** you have created your texture.

Work in as many layers as you want, but avoid the temptation to merge layers. The more your texture workfile retains the individual layers, the better your chances of going back into the file and adjusting later or getting parts for things you may not have thought about yet, such as highlight maps and bump maps.

In our example, four layers exist: the background template, two different rock strata that play off each other, and a layer with fault lines.

To get the main strata lines to roughly follow the surface, the strata layers were edited with the layer set on a 70 percent opacity. This way the background shows through and the work area is clear. If you were working on the airliner and your template was a wing of the plane, you could clearly see the outline of the wing this way, making sure that any detail, such as lines for flaps, were placed in exact locations.

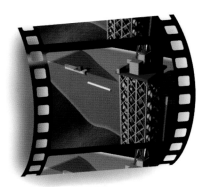

When the editing is done, change all the layers to 100 percent. This should cover up the template– unless you have clear areas in the overlaying layers. To cover the clear areas, create a properly colored "fill" layer just above the background. For instance, your airplane wings may use a white fill that matches the rest of the plane. This preserves your underlying template and allows you to go back and revise it in the future.

After you finish building, you can simply "Save a Copy" and create a flattened file that does not affect the original. With adequate RAM, you may even be able to run your modeling program and import the texture to try it

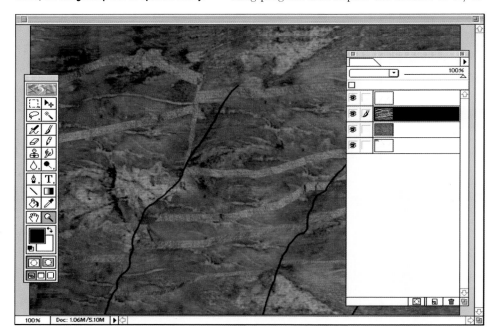

In the strata example, editing in layers allowed the positioning of each element and creation of details such as the faults. By keeping a version with all the layers intact, the image map can be updated easily.

out without leaving Photoshop. Using the "Save a Copy" feature also frees you from unwanted "File In Use" dialog boxes that may occur in some programs. Saving the file as a copy keeps the original on the screen, while a "Save As" makes a new file, but that file will still be in use.

When you are done, you will be able to apply the new texture to the shape and line it up so that the texture you created fits over the shape just like it did in the original template.

This technique obviously works best with flat objects, but also can be applied to other

shapes. While the results may not be as precise with a twisting freeform shape, at least you will have a better feel for how to create the shape than you would just creating it by eye.

For cylindrical objects you can use the previously mentioned technique for the object's height, but you will have to do a little math to figure out the object's circumference. Most programs allow you to create cylinders by entering the shape's desired radius. To figure out how wide a texture map needs to be to wrap around a shape, high school algebra raises its head. Remember $C=2\pi r$? Well that is the key here. If you can determine the radius for your object, then you can do the math on your handy calculator. (All desktop scientific calculators have π functions and several are available online as shareware or freeware–just another tool for the arsenal.) The object's texture width is going to be the object's circumference, so multiply π by the radius doubled and you will get the size. And all this time you have been telling people that those algebra classes were a waste of time!

When creating the texture map, keep in mind the final file size needed to match the output. For video, the final image will be 72 dpi. While this usually requires a simple color map, keep in mind that if you plan to move the camera close to the object, you will have to create a big file or it will pixelate. At the same time, you do not want a 16 megabyte texture map on something that will never be full screen. The rendering time alone will be a killer, but it also will be a bear to work with. For screen-resolution work, keep in mind that the texture map on the object should never get larger than the map in your image editing program at 100 percent view. Any closer and you will get the dreaded pixel blowout.

For print images, you will want to think much bigger. Take a look at that texture map at 100 percent view on your screen and then view it at 25 percent. That 25 percent view is roughly how big the full resolution map will look at 300 dpi. To get that kind of resolution, a tiled map may have to be smaller than you visualized and repetitious tiling may start occurring. If this happens, you may need to be working at a larger scale.

If you are caught in that in between world

EDITING THE TEXTURE MAP

With the template created, bring it into your image editing program (see page 89 "Creating the Template"). Use the template as a guideline so that elements in the texture line up exactly where they need to be.

1

With the template as the background, create a new layer and paste or create the texture maps. In Photoshop (4.0 and later), pasting automatically creates a new layer.

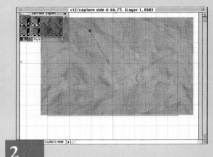

2

To be able to see what you are doing, make the layer slightly transparent. Position your elements and make the layer opaque when done.

3

Use the layers to your advantage. For example, the eraser tool used on a top layer allows the bottom later to come through–done here to establish the strata.

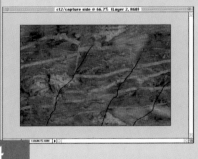

4

When done, crop your image. Do not flatten it. You may want to go back into the texture later, so keep it in layers, using the "Save a Copy" feature to both flatten a copy and preserve your original.

5

One reason to save layers may be to make associated highlight or bump maps. In this case, a copy of the file was saved and converted to grey scale to be used as a bump map.

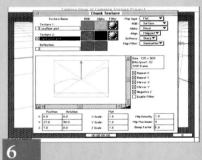

6

Import the final product into your modeling or animation program. Line up the texture map to the object. If you cropped close, you should have no problem setting it up.

where you want to use the same image for both print and video, you may have to reach a compromise and work with a slightly higher image map. While you will definitely pay a price in rendering time, you also may want to increase your anti-aliasing settings as high as possible. That way some of the smaller detail that would have survived on a low resolution map will not get lost in the noise of a more detailed texture.

Also keep the darkness of a texture map in mind when deciding on the scale with which to work. A darker texture map, such as a rock wall, will not only lose some detail when it's reproduced on a smaller scale, but it also can lose any highlights that made it an interesting texture in the first place–and give you a dark, muddy wall, flattening the object.

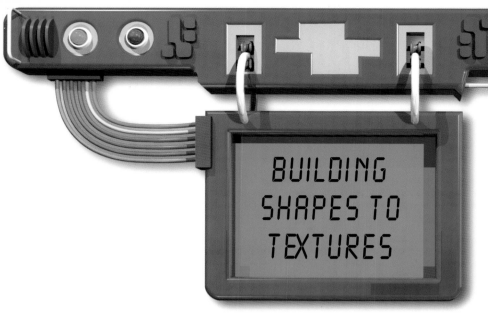

BUILDING SHAPES TO TEXTURES

Form does not always dictate design. Sometimes it is the design that rules, and form has to follow. When creating a model, the texture map may establish how the model looks. In these circumstances, you most likely will be designing the texture map first and then work with the modeling program. Unless you are incredibly gifted in the spatial relations department, it is a good idea to use the results of the texture creation to form the model.

Most modeling programs support using image import as templates, making the process easy for the modeler. As you build your texture, keep in mind that you will be building a shape from the texture. Here are some tips to help make the process a little easier.

Although you could simply import the final image as the template, chances are that your texture will be involved enough to muck up any chances of seeing the actual model through a cluttered texture. For this reason, create a clean, simple template that reflects the form of the object. Export the template as a separate file to be used as a guide in creating the final shape.

When creating a simple tiling texture, work within a square or a rectangle so the results do not require a specific shape to be mapped. Working with a simple shape is one of the joys of tiling textures. But this is not the case with form-specific texture maps. Complicated, form-specific texture maps are often the result of complex layering, paths, and alpha channels. Use these elements to help create the template.

In some cases, you will want to build your model around the texture map shape. As shown below, the monitor shape needed to conform to the image on the screen.

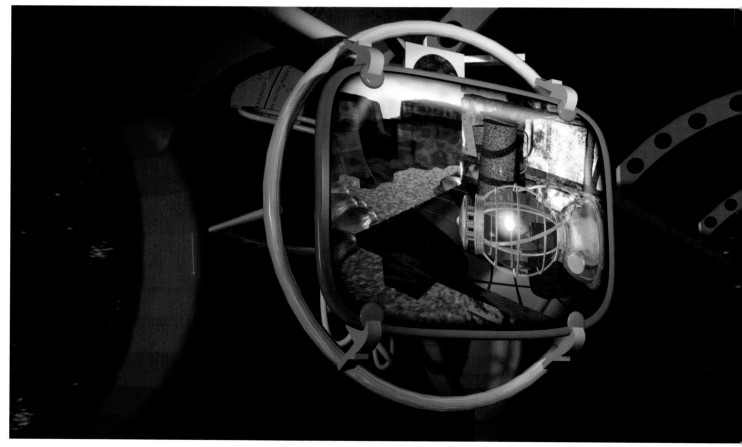

CREATING THE TEMPLATE

In some cases, you will have a texture before the model. In this case, a format was needed to allow the multiple import of video frames at a precise proportion. Then a monitor would be created to fit the images. The first step is creating a template from the texture.

1 Design the texture. As you create the form, save any paths, layers or alpha channels. These may become the building blocks for other parts of the model in the future.

2 Either design an object to serve as the shape you want to use in the modeling program or use an element in your texture for that purpose. In this texture, the rounded rim will be the shape. This was formed by using a path.

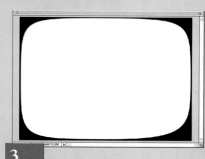

3 Export an image that represents the shape. For this example, we used the path to create an alpha channel and exported the channel as a PICT file to be used as a template.

With a single alpha channel showing the outline of the texture area, you are done. "Copy" the alpha channel, "Paste" it into a new document, and "Save" the file. Now you have your template.

If you have a series of alpha channels and the final result is the outline of the texture, create a new alpha channel and load each previous alpha channel. Delete the selected area until you have a composite of the form area. "Cut" and "Paste" the alpha channel into a new document and you are set.

If you used paths instead of alpha channels, outline the image area and turn the path into a selection. "Save" the selection as an alpha channel and create a template document from that.

Every model presents its own opportunities, so if the above tip does not fit your needs try this: create your own template by using the path tool or a combination of the selection tools to select the area you want to turn into a shape. Make an alpha channel from this area and you are set.

If you have the software to support it, one

other route exists. In Photoshop, if you created your shape using a path, you can export that path using the "Paths to Illustrator..." menu selection to actually export a vector EPS outline. (The command sequence is: "File," "Export," "Paths to Illustrator...") With a program like EPS Invigorator, you can create a shape directly from this path. You are not going to be able to get a better marriage if you use a path to create a texture and the same path to create a shape. With the template created and saved as a format that your modeling program accepts for importing, the first step is done.

Here are a few hints to keep in mind. If the texture map is very small, you may opt to enlarge the template so that it will not be too small when you bring it into your modeling program. If the modeling program uses red or black lines as primary wireframe outlines and your template is red or black, you may not be able to see the wireframe well, therefore, grey values work well as templates.

Where to import your template or underlay? Some modeling programs work in modes

where you construct the shapes in separate workshop windows, and this is where you bring your template or underlay. Other programs allow construction in the main view, and you import your template here. If you are in the whole world (main) view, set your view so that you can draw on a flat template.

In the case of our monitor texture, the view was set to front and then the template was imported as an overlay. The final product is facing in the desired direction without needing to rotate afterwards. The perspective for the view needs to be turned off so you are working in orthographic mode.

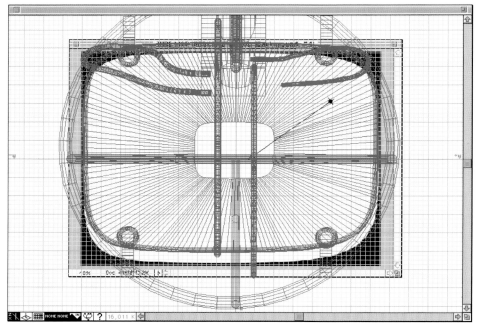

Now it is a matter of tracing the outline of the template to create the form. Be as precise or as loose as your individual texture allows. Set yourself up for success by building in a little latitude with the original texture. With the monitor texture map, we planned a little overlap so that if the texture did not line up exactly with the shape, we would not notice. If your shape is precise, it is a good idea to build the texture slightly larger than the shape so that the texture does not cut into the shape. A solid outer ridge might serve to keep the texture map from streaking in this case. Since the monitor texture was designed with an alpha

channel to act as a decal mask, streaking was not a concern for this project.

We planned for the texture map on the monitor to go on the front of the shape, allowing us to adjust the rest of the shape to become a more desirable form–keeping the front-most shape the same to line up with the texture map. The back points are taper deformed so the monitor tube will begin to take shape, and the front ridge is beveled for a smooth, rounder tube-esque look. When the tweaking is done, the texture map is applied. Using the alpha channel as a decal map and a straight image map, the texture lines up perfectly with the shape.

An additional glow map is applied. The glow map is created at the same time as the original texture on a separate layer. After the main texture is output, the glow map areas are put on top of a field of black and exported as their own file. The resulting file is the same size as the original texture map so all the placement coordinates and scaling information can be transferred from the original texture onto the newly imported glow map. This results in a reflective top edge to the tube that gives it a more realistic look.

In the case of our monitor, the same model is used with several different images on the monitors, so it is key to keep the original workfile without merging the layers. This way the main image can be pasted onto the bottom layer and all the supporting layers above it, including the glow map, will all instantly create a new texture map with minimal work. Even the alpha channel remains to continue its job as a decal mask. When mapped onto the new monitor, the same position, rotation and scale settings carry over.

If for any reason your program does not, cannot, or will not support templates, one last resort–although not as precise–actually works relatively well. Every so often digital artists need to step out of their computer world and do something as odd as taping a sheet of acetate to their screen. With a sheet of acetate on your screen, you can outline the shape of your texture, open up your modeling program and build a form based on the traced area. While being a little less accurate, for some purposes this may be quicker and more than ade-

EDITING THE SHAPE

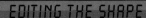

Bring the created template into your modeling program (see page 93 "Creating the Template"). Use the template as a guideline so that elements in the texture line up exactly where they need to be.

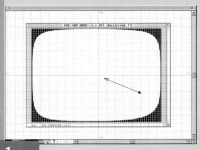

1

Import the texture as a template or an underlay. Most modeling programs support image import for templates. If all else fails, bring it in as a background.

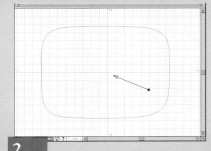

2

Build a shape around the form. In this case a NURB line tool was used to draw the outline in an extruded shape. The result is a shape that fits the texture map.

3

Edit the shape to finish the form. To create the tube feel, the edges were beveled and the shape was deformed to make the back end smaller.

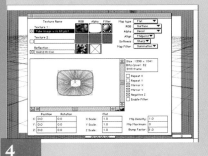

4

Import the original texture map from which the template was created. Apply it to the surface of the model. A straight decal map (above) was used with the alpha channel (shown on previous page) masking the image.

5

Use the same technique for bump and glow maps. Here, a glow map was created for a reflection. The shape followed the textured area and was imported in the same position as the main texture map.

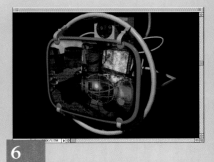

6

Render the results. The final image will give a texture map and solid model shape that work in harmony together.

quate. For this solution, it is a good idea to keep a box of acetate and a Sharpie marker laying around. Many times during both the modeling and texture-building periods you might want a quick reference for placement of objects. This method is one of the quickest ways to get there. Static electricity usually holds the film to the screen. Falling short of that, you can use masking tape.

This technique can be applied to elements of creating animations as well. It is a painless way of quickly marking off areas that won't fall into a video viewing area (usually 1/2 an inch around the edges of a 640x480 screen area), and for loosely positioning elements for animations—sort of an acetate story board where you can note the relative positions of objects.

CREATING A BUILDING FACADE

In that moment when the camera pans by a building, you want it to look realistic. But the prospect of constructing a building from scratch for a couple of seconds is daunting. One way around this hurdle is to create a texture map using a photograph of a building and then map the results on a simple shape. This solution renders quickly and gives you a realistic building.

When building an architectural scene, you have three choices: build it from scratch, fake it and slap texture-mapped facades on everything, or combine the first two methods. While you may need the detail that building from scratch provides, facades should not be discounted.

Even in the real world, facades are a standard device to copy the look without breaking the budget. The classic example is paneling.

Some paneling and tiles are created in a process where actual photographs of real surfaces are printed onto less expensive plywood and tile. So if this works for the real world, modelers should take advantage of the process as well.

The biggest benefit—other than not modeling all the incredible detail—is rendering time. To make the process work, invest some of your saved time in making a detailed facade.

A detailed facade can be created by designing the facade from scratch in an image editing program such as Photoshop; building a model from scratch of a single facade section destined for tiling later; photographing a building and using the photo as an image map; or purchasing the facade from a third party.

If you are going to build a facade, work a little larger than you anticipate the image to be. This gives you more flexibility in the future. If you decide to move the camera closer to a building, you will want to have the option of importing the larger texture.

BUILDING A BUILDING

Very few building facades are flat. Most have sills and insets. Building a model with all these details creates an extremely complex model with a long render time. Designing a facade in Photoshop helps give you the detail you need without the huge polygon count.

1

Start with the base color. Make a field larger than you expect to need as the tiling frame. This gives you a larger canvas to use.

2

Many building facades have inset window frames. Create this effect from scratch or, as above, use Eye Candy's inside bevel tool.

3

Select the window area and give it color. Stroke the selection to give the window frame more of an edge. Save the selection for later.

4

Punch up the surface detail if you want a grainy, stucco or concrete feel. To do this, apply the Noise filter followed by Gallery Effects' Emboss tool.

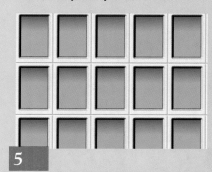

5

Select the window area and use it to define a pattern. Create a new document and fill it with the pattern to test how the final facade will look.

6

If the results are good, crop the original frame. You may want to scale it down if your final building will not be too large.

7

To add reflection to the window, open the saved window selection alpha channel. "Inverse" the alpha channel. "Select All," "Copy," and "Paste" into a new document.

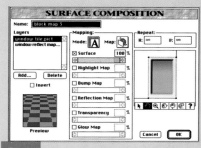

8

Apply the surface to your object (a simple flat plane or a cube). Composite the reflection map at the same time.

9

The final result is a quick building with lots of detail that renders quickly.

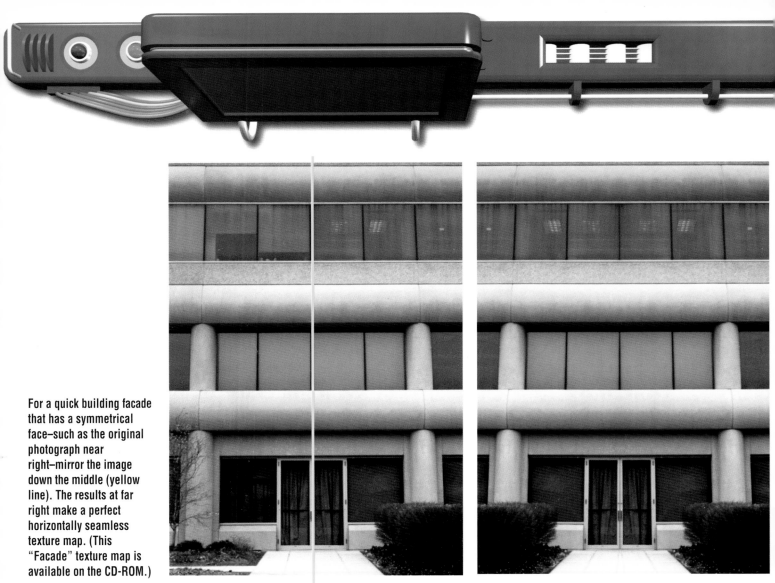

For a quick building facade that has a symmetrical face–such as the original photograph near right–mirror the image down the middle (yellow line). The results at far right make a perfect horizontally seamless texture map. (This "Facade" texture map is available on the CD-ROM.)

Keep all channels and paths as you build. Some of this information may be useful later. An example–as shown on the previous page–is using the area for the window as a reflection map. The same image map could be used as a transparency map if you wanted to actually see through the facade. Filters help in the process of creating surfaces. Experiment with the filters that ship with Photoshop (such as the Noise and Emboss used in the example) or invest in a third party filter set (such as Kai's Power Tools, Paint Alchemy or Eye Candy.)

Bevels can create the illusion of depth for inset windows or creases in structures. Remember, if the facade will be tiled, avoid doing anything that causes a noticeable, unintended repeating pattern. An example here might be a lens flare on the window. While one lens flare may look cool, when repeated 50 times, it kills the texture of the building.

Also keep in mind that your final result needs to tile seamlessly. If you are building from scratch, it is pretty easy to maintain a continual background surface that will tile when you are done. To make sure, check the tile by selecting the area and defining it as a pattern. This pattern then can be used to fill a larger, new document and gives you instant feedback on the success of the tiling. If you have any problems you can get a correct tile by following the procedure on page 74.

Another way to create a detailed facade is to render a model of a portion of a building and use it as a texture map for tiling on a larger surface. Remember that the final purpose is for mapping onto a flat surface. After creating the model, render out the final scene in an orthographic mode without perspective or in a telephoto setting so that the perspective will not be too extreme. Bring the final output into an image editing program. Check to make sure the edges all continue across, up, and down for a proper tile. Save the textures you used to create the initial model. You may use these flat

USING PHOTOGRAPHS FOR FACADES

Creating a facade from a photograph gives realistic results, yet allows the artist to edit and customize the texture map. You can scan in a photograph or, if you do not have a scanner available, you can have your film digitized onto a Kodak CD-ROM.

1 Take the photograph. Try to pick a slightly overcast day. Mid-day gives even shadows. Shoot as straight-on as possible with a tele-photo lens.

2 Scan the image. Crop as needed, leaving a little extra room on the sides. This allows you to change the image's perspective later.

3 In an image editing program that supports layers (such as Photoshop), create a new layer. Draw horizontal and vertical lines along important elements, such as the window.

4 Use the selection tool to choose an area outside of the area you plan to include in the final edit. Use the distortion feature under the "Transform" menu and drag the edges on the image to correct the perspective of the main level.

5 Crop the image to include only the perspective corrected area. Tile the edges (see page 74) so that the sides mirror each other to create a seamless tiling map. Save the image.

6 Map the texture onto the surface. The result should be a seamless wall of windows.

textures in later modeling of the surface to extend an area beyond the tiled model image.

The most realistic and customized of all the detailed facade creation methods is photographing existing buildings. With a digital camera, it is easier to bring the images into the computer. Most of us do not have a digital camera. But most 35mm cameras suffice. If you do not have access to a scanner, you can shoot off a roll of film and send it to a photo processor who can put the images on a CD-ROM.

If you can plan when you go out to shoot the photographs, try to pick a slightly overcast day. The light on an overcast day is more diffused and the shadows are less harsh. Try taking pictures during mid-day, keeping long, angular, horizontal shadows from forming.

The key to using photographs as image maps is perspective correction. You will have to shift perspective a little—unless you can get at a vantage point that puts you square on with the architectural element or you have a

perspective correcting lens (few of us do.) If you photograph a building standing on the ground, the top of a window is going to be smaller than the bottom.

Here is a pretty straightforward way to correct perspective. Open the photographed image in Photoshop. By default, the image is the background layer. Create a new layer and double click on your "Line" tool. Choose a thin line (one or two pixels). Pick a foreground color that will not get lost in your photograph (bright yellow). On this new layer, draw a line from the widest point on the left side of the window's base (or whatever architectural feature you are manipulating) and, holding down the "Shift" key to constrain, draw a line up to the top of the window. This line gives you a feel for straight perspective. Do this again on the right side. If the horizontal lines are a little crooked, you might want to do this with the top and bottom sides as well.

Now select the background layer with the building image. Choose an area wider than the final area you plan to crop. Use the "Transform/Distort" tool to pull the top corner handles out to the sides. Work with the handles until the sides of the windows line up with your grid lines. When you are done, hit the "Enter" key to perform the distortion.

Crop the image so none of the non-distorted area is in the new area. You will find that other elements, like bricks, line up. Crop so the image looks like it will tile well and then use the pattern testing and seamless tiling techniques to check the tile.

A single image from the side of a building can be used on two separate models to create a more realistic model. For instance, the building (below) could be mapped directly onto the side of the plank with believable results, especially if you zip the camera by quickly.

If you are planning to spend more time on an area, you might want to do something that increases the realism of the scene without killing yourself in modeling or rendering time. A way to do this is to build a flat plank with the whole scene on it. Then create a second plank with holes cut where the windows are located. The result will be an inset window that gives the scene a little depth, provides a little shadow and makes the scene a little more believable.

Use the same technique for other elements of a digital urban landscape. Details such as doorways and signs on the sides of buildings can be applied the same way. Most modeling programs allow for multiple texture maps to be applied. If this is your situation, one layer can

The facade itself cannot carry an image. Simple roof detail helps make the picture complete. Details such as air ducts, vents and antenna can be made with primitive objects, keeping rendering to a minimum. This is important if building a whole city.

CREATING BI-LEVEL FACADES

A single flat texture on a single flat shape may look good and render fast, but as you move to the side, the flatness of the object becomes more obvious. A trick around this is described below.

1 Take the photograph and edit it to correct perspective. Make it a seamless tile, as described on page 74.

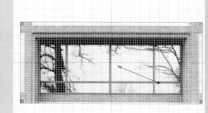

2 Following the technique described on page 92, build the outer facade using the texture map as a template so the window hole is in the proper place.

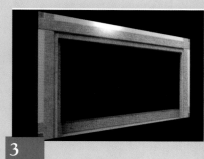

3 Apply the texture to the shape in your modeling program. There should be a hole where the window glass should be.

4 Using the same technique as Step 2, build the same facade or use the same elements for the window shape in your modeling program, but remove the hole in the middle so it is a solid shape.

5 Apply the texture using the same position, scale and rotation parameters as the texture applied in Step 3.

6 Bring the two models together, centering the shapes onto each other. Set the solid shape back a little, insetting the window glass and creating a more dimensional facade.

have the windows, another a photograph of a parking sign and yet another layer might have a doorway. You can construct an entire building with three texture maps and a simple shape.

The last detailed facade method may require parting with hard-earned cash. Artbeats sells a very competent set of win-dows and other urban landscape items in a package called City Surfaces. These images come in both high and low resolutions for video/multimedia work and print. This book's companion CD-ROM also includes a handful of home-grown building facade textures.

INCLUDING SOUND TRACKS IN ANIMATIONS

An important element to animation creation is sound. Your audience may be impressed by a sharp animation, but they will not be completely drawn into it and will not experience the animation fully if it does not have a soundtrack to compliment it.

Sound is an elusive animal. Without it, animations seem flat. But when sound is included, you want to make it so natural, so fitting, that you hardly notice it. Sounds surround us every waking second, but we filter them out and accept their presence to the point where we may not focus on them. Yet when sound is absent, we notice. It is important to follow through with a sound track that supports the images you are creating, yet does not distract.

Sounds fall into two major areas: ambient and reaction. Ambient sounds might be viewed as the environment map of the sound world. In a space scene, the ambient sound is

the low rumble of the mother ship. Or, in a landscape scene, it might be the chirping of a bird, even though you might not see the bird. Ambient sounds give you a more rounded sense of placement.

Reaction sounds are the sounds we hear when an event happens—a plane blows up, a frog hops in a pond or a gong is hit. If you had an animation with any of these events happening without an accompanying sound track, the whole scene would lack something, no matter how wonderful the animation.

In some situations, animators do not have to spend time worrying about sound. It is another department's job. Most of us do not have that luxury and it's just as well, because playing with sounds can be a lot of fun. Planning sounds along with the rest of your animation can make a well-rounded production. Creating desktop productions allows a range of creative efforts to be produced often with only an additional program or two. Sound effects fit perfectly into the comfortable realm of "cool-things-I-can-do-with-my-computer."

Working with sound is similar to working with other elements in animation. In terms of time, sound is a linear thing just like an animation. In terms of content, sound is an element that can be manipulated over time or filtered and edited just like an animation.

EDITING SOUNDS

To work effectively with sounds you need a few things. The first is a sound editing pro-

Programs like DECK II (at right) offer an incredible amount of control over sound for animations. Software-based mixing systems mimic hardware setups found previously only in studios and produce CD-quality audio tracks since everything you work with is digital. Working in unison with waveform editors, these mixing programs can add the impressive final touch of realism that animations demand.

SYNCHRONIZING SOUNDS AND ANIMATIONS

Sound Forge for Windows and SoundEdit for Macintosh synchronize audio with video using thumbnail images. These can be hard to read and do not show every frame, making sound placement difficult. A way around this is to output a small version of the animation with visual tags.

1 Create the animation. Edit the files as needed in a video or animation editing program.

2 Create an image file to import into your editing program that will act as a marker to indicate where your sounds start or stop.

3 Open your image editing program and find the spot where you want to begin the soundtrack.

4 Import the image file you created. In this example, since it is just a layer in the movie, it can be deleted when you are finished. Output the movie as a small, quarter- or third-sized movie.

5 Import the movie into your sound editing program. Even if the thumbnail image is small, you will see the location of where you want to begin the sound.

6 Design the soundtrack around your markers. Output the final file as a single, mixed soundtrack. Import it into your video editing program. The sounds will line up where they should.

gram. The second handy item is a sound-input device on your computer to import any custom sounds you might want.

Beyond the sound editing programs available, a search of shareware libraries on the Web turns up many usable and inexpensive programs for Windows and Macintosh. It is possible to skip sound editing programs and work with your editing program since some animation and video editing programs—such as After Effects and Premiere—allow for a reasonable amount of control over sounds. But most of these video editing programs involve placement and volume of sounds in the production. Sometimes a sound file is not exactly what you want until you adjust it a little. This is when you need your sound editing program.

Working with sounds is similar to editing an image in Photoshop. You can crop, change the size, change the resolution (sampling

rate), enhance and filter the sound just like you could a photo. If your sound has elements you do not want, you can crop. If you need the sound to play a little longer, you can stretch it out over time. If the sound is creating too large a file size, you can sample it down and if you want to clean up some buzzing noise, you can run it through a noise gate filter. Yet these alterations barely scratch the surface of what a sound editing program can do.

If you plan on including a lot of sounds in your production, consider a program like Sound Forge for Windows or SoundEdit for the Mac. These programs allow you to view your animation file (AVI for Sound Forge, QuickTime for SoundEdit) in the sound program so you can carefully synchronize your soundtrack to the action going on in the program. While you can do this with a good degree of success in your animation editing program, working within your sound editing program while looking at events allows you to fine-tune and finesse the file easily and achieve precise effects at the right moments.

GETTING SOUNDS
Sounds come in a variety of packages. Sounds can be generated by using a microphone that comes with your computer, down-

loaded off of the Web, purchased from a multimedia sound supplier or created with your own equipment. All Macintoshes are sound capable. If you plan to work with high-quality multimedia productions, make sure your Mac is capable of 16-bit sound input. Most PCs ship with sound cards that allow for sound input. Make sure your PC is capable of 16-bit sound input. Even if you plan to sample the sounds down to 8-bit later, the overall quality will be better if you start with 16-bit audio.

As a rule, microphones that ship with computers are a little on the flaky side. So if you plan on recording a lot of narration on your computer, investigate the better quality microphones to determine what is best.

A direct patch from your stereo into your computer can be an ideal solution for many users. This allows you to pre-amplify your microphone if you were not pleased with the direct microphone to computer sound. Patching through your stereo also allows input sounds from cassettes, CD-ROMs and even phonographs. Since many people have already invested money in a nice stereo system, why not use it in your computer sound system? This option also allows experimentation with changing the audio level, balance and tone adjustments before inputting into your computer.

If your sound input uses a stereo RCA-type plug, all you need to do is to run a patch cable between your stereo output and the computer. If you have a stereo mini-pin on your computer, you can buy an RCA-to-mini-pin Y-adapter at your local electronics store. If you have mono input, run your left stereo RCA output to your computer using an RCA-to-mini-pin cable, making sure your stereo is set to mono. If you have an electrical musical instrument, you can patch that into your computer as well. Those connections, as well as general MIDI topics are covered on page 107.

Tons of sounds are available on-line. On-line services such as America On-line and CompuServe have forums dedicated to electronic sound and music. Both have libraries full of audio files and most are saved in formats that sound editing programs can read. A search for "Sound" on the Web shows several sites

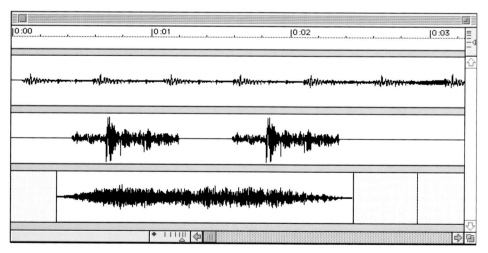

Much like multi-track editing with video clips, sound editing is done in layers. Most sound editing programs work the same, giving the viewers a look at the sound's wave form for editing. Just like compositing layered animations, when the final edit is done the multiple layers are mixed into one track, or two for stereo.

ANIMATION TIPS AND TRICKS

where public domain sound files are available. Even if you cannot find the exact sound you are looking for, you may be able to download a similar sound, adjust it in your sound editing program and get the desired sound.

Music tracks also are available that serve as good ambient noise. If you are creating sound files for your own *personal* productions, you will find short samples of many movie sound bites, but it might be a stretch to find the right place to use quips from *Caddy Shack*. Be respectful of copyrights. Many of the available on-line samples cross the border of copyright infringement.

If you are serious about animation, then you need to be serious about sounds. Buying a library of sound effects is a good investment. Several companies offer sound effects libraries. The range of available sound effects spans from some inexpensive CD-ROMs available from companies like Educorps to others from high-end companies that have extensive libraries and offer thousands of sounds. Sound Ideas offers a well-rounded sound effects bundle of 40 disks with 6,000 or so sounds in a package called General for about $1,500. They also offer a small but useful collection on their SFX CD-ROM (some samples of their collection can be found on this book's CD-ROM). Janus Interactive offers a reasonably priced package of approximately 5,000 sound effects. If you shop around, you can find budget multimedia CD-ROMs with thousands of sounds for less than $20. But remember, you get what you pay for.

The Sound Ideas' General collection comes in standard CD-audio format and ships with a Disc-to-Disk utility that converts the sound tracks to compatible multimedia sound files, like WAV or SND files. If you are doing character animation, you might be interested in Sound Ideas' collection of Hanna-Barbara soundtracks. The collection also includes libraries that focus on ambient sounds, cars and Hollywood. Most other companies ship their files with browsers that can save in the format of your choice. Some sound editing packages ship with small but well-rounded libraries.

Background music is considered an ambi-

ent sound and is treated in the same manner as the other sound effects. In many cases, just adding a music background to an animation brings the production to life. People are used to intense multimedia experiences due to their exposure to videos, television and movies. Underlying music usually is present and often required, yet it does not have to be loud–just present. What would the movie *Jaws* be like without the DAHN-NAHN, DAHN-NAHN track, or a *Star Wars* X-Wing Fighter scene without the DAH-NA-NA-NA, DAH-NA-NA beat? You get the point.

Using music from your audio CD collection is possible, but is illegal and generally in bad taste. Companies like Sound Ideas offer production mix CD-ROMs with copyright-free sound-alikes that serve the same purpose of setting the pulse or tone to an animation. If you are creating a high-end production, you might consider having a studio create a sound track for you. If they can one-off (create a single CD) for you, then you can bring the file right into your computer. Several utilities are available for converting audio-CDs to multimedia sound files, and programs such as SoundEdit can do the task internally.

When working in sound, keep your final output in mind. If you can save your files as high resolution (16-bit, 44 khz), then everything you do is bound to sound sharp and crisp. If you are sampling the files down for CD-ROM or Web output (8-bit, 11khz) things begin to get scratchy fast. Breathing or a jet flying can both sound like annoying static when sampled down. Try out a sound first and see if it works when it is sampled down.

Sound files can get very big very fast which is why compression schemes are available. But just like image files, there is no free lunch. Size reduction comes out of somewhere and the highly compressed sound files can sound choppy and grainy. While this might be fine for some reaction sounds–like a plane blowing up or a ping-pong ball bouncing–it kills the effect you might be trying to achieve with an ambient sound. In some cases, you may just have to edit the ambient sound out if you are trying to get a really small file.

USING MIDI TO CREATE SOUND EFFECTS

If you were told you could pick up 7,808 sound effects for a few hundred bucks, you would think it was a good deal. If the same investment were to produce 60,964,864 sound effects, you would be in heaven. Well, the good news is that this purchase is possible and more readily available than you might think. You can even go down to your local electronic or music store and pick it up right now. This answer to your audio prayers is a basic electronic keyboard.

Keyboards that tie into your animations come in two flavors: ones that have some type of audio-out (either headphone jacks or AUX-out plugs) or full-fledged MIDI configurations. The key is finding the right combination of cables and adapters to go between your keyboard and your sound board or computer sound input. These over-the-counter adapters are readily available and you should be able to configure something without splicing any wires. A common configuration is a cable that has a 1/4" plug on one end and an RCA plug on the other, which would plug into the computer. Any possible combination is possible. If the keyboard has a single headphone plug, that plug will be stereo, so you will either need an adapter that splits off to the right and left inputs on your computer. Or if you have a single-pin input on your computer, a simple adapter might do. The number of possibilities are too numerous to cover, but the concept is simple. If in doubt, ask the folks selling the cables. They will be able to tell you what you need.

With that done, you can record your audio by either using the systems sound recorder–both Windows and Mac ship with their own versions–or you should use a sound editing package. Most keyboards have 128 standard voices

GENERAL MIDI SYSTEM

Instruments and devices that carry this label conform to General MIDI standards and will work with programs and systems regardless of manufacturer.

MUSICAL INSTRUMENT DIGITAL INTERFACE...

You cannot just walk into a store and ask for a MIDI (Musical Instrument Digital Interface). Well, you could, but you would look a little silly. MIDI is to the music world what Postscript is to the art world. A flute player has no need for MIDI to play the flute well and a watercolor artist has no need for Postscript to paint well. Once each of those artists begins dabbling in the digital world, however, they will be keenly interested in the digital formats with which they can work.

MIDI is a standard established in 1983, that allows musicians to connect different brands of synthesizers. The language that was created covers a wide range of variables including notes, velocity, pitch blend, aftertouch and the various voices available (see chart on page 109).

Most people usually envision MIDI devices as electronic keyboards, but in reality the keyboard is simply one way to provide input into the device's synthesizer. Sound modules provide the same sound-generating capability but rely on other devices, such as a computer with MIDI software, to provide the input.

The MIDI power for animators can be found in some of the software tools available. Animators are used to working in a linear, format time line when sequencing and editing animations. Music scores work the same way. Working in a program–Studio for Windows or MusicShop for Macs–animators can lay down several tracks of ambient sounds and sound effects to match up with their animations. Those tracks can then be played back and recorded as wave form sound files that can be incorporated into the final animation or into multimedia files.

SETTING UP A MIDI SYSTEM

In its simplest form, a MIDI system consists of a MIDI interface (either a separate box for a Mac or already on a PC sound board), a set of cables and a MIDI instrument, like a keyboard. Software to run the system can be downloaded as shareware or bought off the

1 PC MIDI setup is a bit more complicated than Mac, but the concept is the same and both are easy. First, plug your audio input cables into the sound input port on the sound board.

2 You will listen to your MIDI output through your MIDI device, but you can still use your speakers. Connect speakers to the audio output port on your sound card.

3 Using a universal set of MIDI cables, plug the MIDI adapter cable into the 15-pin joystick port in your sound card.

4 Plug the cables leading from your audio input into the "AUX OUT" port on the MIDI device. This allows you to play on the instrument and record–as a waveform sound file–the output. The output can be used in animations and other multimedia purposes.

5 Plug the cable labeled "MIDI IN" into the instrument's "MIDI OUT" port, and plug the cable's "MIDI OUT" plug into the "MIDI IN" port on the instrument.

6 Make sure your card's drivers are set up to handle the MIDI configuration. Buy or download a MIDI editing program or MIDI player. Your imagination is your only limitation!

and any number of annoying repetitive song styles. If your keyboard has 61 keys, then you can generate 7,808 tones or sounds. If you play any two of those tones on top of each other, then you get the 60 million number.

The sounds generated by a keyboard are not only musical. They cover a wide variety of audio effects and some even have special effects such as gun shots and helicopters. Even the standard musical notes can be toyed with to create some interesting sounds. Playing an

extremely low note on the tremolo strings creates a fantastic "mothership" sound. The percussion instruments provide a wonderful variety of sound elements from hand claps to cow bells.

Even with no musical talent, you can strike a few chords on the "Angel's voice" setting to add a nice ambient feel to an animation or a multimedia presentation. Even straight musical notes can be brought into a sound editing program and tweaked to come up with some interesting effects. A handful of sounds created

by this method can be found on this book's CD-ROM.

A more advanced approach to take with a keyboard is using the Musical Instrument Digital Interface–MIDI. If you are not into music, MIDI can seem like a mystical thing that belongs to recording studios and one-man-bands at the Holiday Inn. This really could not be further from the truth. All you need is a keyboard with general MIDI capability, a $15 cable, and some readily available shareware. The variables all depend on what platform you are using and what you want to do with the setup.

Most sound cards that work with Windows setups have a MIDI port built-in. If this is your situation, all you need for a simple MIDI setup is a cable that runs from your 15-pin joystick port on your sound card to your MIDI-IN and MIDI-OUT ports. These cables can be found at computer stores or at music stores that deal with electronic instruments. Usually the plug marked "IN" goes into your MIDI-OUT port on your keyboard. The plug marked "OUT" goes into the MIDI-IN port. If your sound board does not support MIDI,

then you can buy a MIDI board. PC-based MIDI boards start at about $50.

On the Mac you will need to buy a MIDI interface. This is a small box that attaches to one of your serial ports and allows for MIDI connections. You will need to buy a MIDI cable to run between the box and the keyboard. Most interfaces come with a "THRU" port that allows you to remain connected to your modem, network or printer.

Once you have installed the hardware, it is time for fun. MIDI allows you to control the keyboard from the computer or the computer from the keyboard. If you search around the Web, you will find several shareware MIDI player programs and plug-ins. For instance, if you have a MIDI plug-in for Netscape, you can visit sites with MIDI soundtracks and hear the sound the way it was meant to be, not using the cheesey FM sound synthesis chip in your computer.

If you buy or download a sequencing or composing program, you can actually write music and have it play back on your keyboard. You also can play notes on your keyboard and have it recorded by the software. The final product is still a MIDI file and needs to be converted to an audiowave file so you can include it into your production. Here are three ways to do this: you can use a software package such as MIDI Render to convert a MIDI file to a soundwave form file; you can have one computer play the file while another records the audio output as described earlier in the chapter; or, if your computer can handle it, run the MIDI program while running a sound recording program at the same time. The result is a soundwave file that you can edit digitally and incorporate into your production.

One other boon to animators working by themselves is that they can have someone create a MIDI file for them and e-mail the document to them. MIDI files are incredibly small and lengthy songs take less than a minute to download even with a slow connection. MIDI documents follow a pretty solid standard. Even though creations sound slightly different from one keyboard to another, they remain pretty faithful to the overall score.

MIDI soundtracks that you can find on the Web–and there are thousands–are often writ-

Even if you are not a musician, you can always tap into the wide range of sound elements available on most keyboards. Hundreds of "voices" are accessible on even low-end synthesizers. If you are not interested in the music possibilities, you could work with a non-MIDI system and wire it into your sound card to access the wide range of sounds a keyboard can produce.

ten from scores for popular music and have the same copyright concerns. Using them in commercial productions would be in poor taste. You might find some scores written by individuals who would be interested in having them included in a multimedia production and who might be willing to deal.

An entire world of MIDI instruments and devices exists. For most animators, a simple patch between a keyboard's audio-out port will be all that you need. Animator's who are willing to go further will be treated to a new world of creativity that will help bring their multimedia productions to life.

The chart below shows the voices available in the General MIDI world. Many non-MIDI instruments have the same lineup. You can tap into them simply by connecting a keyboard to your computer sound input.

PIANO	BASS	REED	SYNTH EFFECTS
1. Acoustic Grand Piano	33. Acoustic Bass	65. Soprano Sax	97. FX 1 (rain)
2. Bright Acoustic Piano	34. Electric Bass (finger)	66. Alto Sax	98. FX 2 (soundtrack)
3. Electric Grand Piano	35. Electric Bass (pick)	67. Tenor Sax	99. FX 3 (crystal)
4. Honky-tonk Piano	36. Fretless Bass	68. Baritone Sax	100. FX 4 (atmosphere)
5. Electric Piano 1	37. Slap Bass 1	69. Oboe	101. FX 5 (brightness)
6. Electric Piano 2	38. Slap Bass 2	70. English Horn	102. FX 6 (goblins)
7. Harpsichord	39. Synth Bass 1	71. Bassoon	103. FX 7 (echoes)
8. Clavi	40. Synth Bass 2	72. Clarinet	104. FX 8 (sci-fi)
CHROM PERC	STRINGS	PIPE	ETHNIC
9. Celesta	41. Violin	73. Piccolo	105. Sitar
10. Glockenspiel	42. Viola	74. Flute	106. Banjo
11. Music Box	43. Cello	75. Recorder	107. Shamisen
12. Vibraphone	44. Contrabass	76. Pan Flute	108. Koto
13. Marimba	45. Tremolo Strings	77. Blown Bottle	109. Kalimba
14. Xylophone	46. Pizzicato Strings	78. Shakuhachi	110. Bag Pipe
15. Tubular Bells	47. Orchestral Harp	79. Whistle	111. Fiddle
16. Dulcimer	48 Timpani	80. Ocarina	112. Shanai
ORGAN	ENSEMBLE	SYNTH LEAD	PERCUSSIVE
17. Drawbar Organ	49. String Ensemble 1	81. Lead 1 (square)	113. Tinkle Bell
18. Percussive Organ	50. String Ensemble 2	82. Lead 2 (sawtooth)	114. Agogo
19. Rock Organ	51. SynthStrings 1	83. Lead 3 (calliope)	115. Steel Drums
20. Church Organ	52. SynthStrings 2	84. Lead 4 (chiff)	116. Woodblock
21. Reed Organ	53. Choir Aahs	85. Lead 5 (charang)	117. Taiko Drum
22. Accordion	54. Voice Oohs	86. Lead 6 (voice)	118. Melodic Tom
23. Harmonica	55. Synth Voice	87. Lead 7 (fifths)	119. Synth Drum
24. Tango Accordion	56. Orchestra Hit	88. Lead 8 (bass + lead)	120. Reverse Cymbal
GUITAR	BRASS	SYNTH PAD	SOUND EFFECTS
25. Acoustic Guitar (nylon)	57. Trumpet	89. Pad 1 (new age)	121. Guitar Fret Noise
26. Acoustic Guitar (steel)	58. Trombone	90. Pad 2 (warm)	122. Breath Noise
27. Electric Guitar (jazz)	59. Tuba	91. Pad 3 (polysynth)	123. Seashore
28. Electric Guitar (clean)	60. Muted Trumpet	92. Pad 4 (choir)	124. Bird Tweet
29. Electric Guitar (muted)	61. French Horn	93. Pad 5 (bowed)	125. Telephone Ring
30. Overdriven Guitar	62. Brass Section	94. Pad 6 (metallic)	126. Helicopter
31. Distortion Guitar	63. SynthBrass 1	95. Pad 7 (halo)	127. Applause
32. Guitar Harmonics	64. SynthBrass 2	96. Pad 8 (sweep)	128. Gunshot

CREATING LIQUID AND FOG MOTION

Liquid and fog effects, often difficult to recreate realistically in modeling programs, can be generated during animation editing.

After creating the main scene where the liquid or fog is used, create a 2D image file to be used as the fluid object. To do this, use your 3D skills by first creating a rough, bumpy terrain model in a modeling program. Adjust the reflection and lights to give rolling highlights. Next, create a surface for the shape that reflects the feel of the fluid you are creating. For water or fog (or smoke), use varying shades of blue or grey. A Gaussian blur provides a softer look. Render out the terrain scene from a top view. Make the image large because during the animation, the file moves over time. The terrain needs to be large enough to allow for a shift in the time and distance required.

Now use an animation editing program, such as After Effects or Premiere. To assemble your fluid or fog animation, start with the base image–the original object scene you rendered. (In the example, it is the veins and arteries on top of the heart.) On top of the base image, place the rendered terrain surface. On another layer, place a duplicate of the surface and rotate it so the highlighted colors are in different locations. Change the mode of this second layer to "lighten" or "luminance," giving more depth to the fluid.

On top of these three layers, place a copy of the base image to be masked. To create the mask, use either an alpha channel mask or, if the editing program supports it, a masking tool. (A feathered edge completes the effect.) The mask openings on this fourth layer become the areas where the fluid or fog flows. For example, create openings where water might flow or the fog might roll in.

Over time, move the two layers, shifting the position and, possibly, the rotation. The top fluid level, set at lightest, plays off the colors of the lower fluid layer, creating a smooth, undulating, flowing feel.

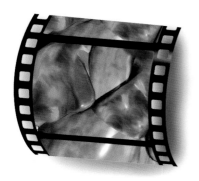

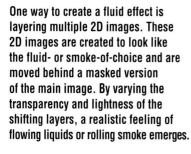

One way to create a fluid effect is layering multiple 2D images. These 2D images are created to look like the fluid- or smoke-of-choice and are moved behind a masked version of the main image. By varying the transparency and lightness of the shifting layers, a realistic feeling of flowing liquids or rolling smoke emerges.

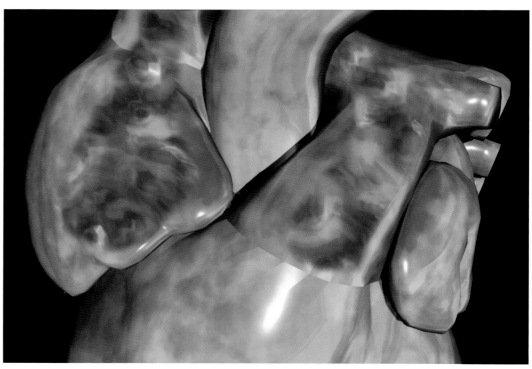

SETTING UP THE X-RAY EFFECT

Half the work of creating an X-ray effect is done in carefully setting up the models. The other half is done in compositing the images, which can be done in Photoshop using layering tools.

1
Start by building the main scene in which the fluid or gas will be used. In our example, we want to show the flow of blood to and from the heart.

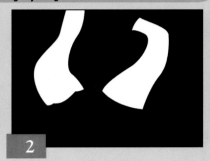

2
Working with a still animation frame, create an image file with an alpha channel to act as a mask to display the area you want to show. Feather the edges for a more realistic feel.

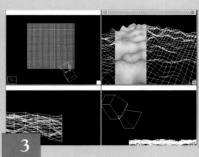

3
Create your liquid image by making a bumpy terrain surface. Adjust the lights so shadows are formed in the valleys. Keep the overall depth shallow.

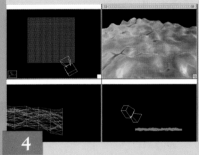

4
Apply a surface color to the terrain. To mimic blood, a marble procedural color was used, playing between light and dark reds. For water, the same technique would work with blue shades.

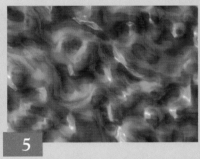

5
Render the scene from the top view. Make sure it is big. The final render is used to shift over time in position to create the flow.

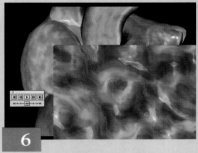

6
In your editing program, such as Premiere or After Effects, import the main scene, then the terrain render.

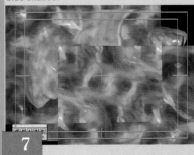

7
Import a copy of the same terrain file. Rotate it 180-degrees and change the ink mode to lightest. This allows the two terrain levels to play off each other. Adjust transparency levels to achieve the right look.

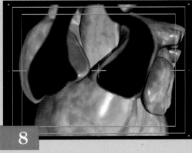

8
On top of the three layers, bring in your main scene with the alpha channel mask, or create a feathered mask if your program supports it.

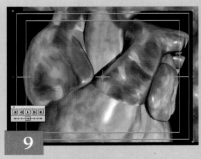

9
Shift the two terrain layers over time. Moving one layer slightly faster and in a slightly different direction enhances the effect.

COMPOSITING ANIMATIONS ONTO VIDEO

The incredible strides in desktop video over the past few years have made video production on the desktop computer not only possible, but commonplace. Not long ago, anyone editing video on a personal computer was considered either a hack or an amateur. Desktop video hardware from Media 100, Targa, Perception, Avid, and Radius–fueled by powerful programs like Premiere, After Effects, and Speed Razor–give the people who create 3D animations the ability to take the final product and record it to tape without having to leave the desktop. And the street is two-way: animators now can tap into these same programs to bring video into their animations, or to composite their animations into the video.

Keep a few considerations in mind if you are planing to merge these two worlds. The most important fundamental is that both sources, video and animation, are speaking the same language. Since the final product can go one of two ways, for video or for computer playback, you will want to make sure that both source files conform to the final product. For instance, if your final product is for broadcast video, you will want to make sure you capture your video to composite at video specifications, namely an interlaced video running at 30 frames per second. When you are setting up your animation, you will want to make sure you follow the same guidelines. This way when the two are brought together, you will not have any surprises.

If your final product is destined for CD-ROM or computer playback, you may opt for a slower frame rate such as 15 frames per second, and a file that would be non-interlaced. Setting both your video capture and your animation output to match will insure proper fit.

The size of the screen also is a factor. For working with video you will want to work with the manufacturer's suggestions, which are often either 640 x 480 pixels or 720 x 540. If your program gives you the option, you want to be working with square pixels.

If your final product is for CD-ROM and uses a smaller screen such as 320 x 240, you may want to work at the larger 640 x 480 size and scale the final production down when you are done. Doing this increases your rendering time, but it also gives you more flexibility later. If your production is long, say five or 10 minutes, then there might be advantages to working smaller, since the rendering time and the final file size will be significantly smaller.

Do not shoot the video as an afterthought to the animation you are working on. It is best to shoot the video, digitize it, and use it as a background file while you are working. This allows you to check perspectives and positions.

If your system cannot handle the overhead of importing a huge video file, a couple alternatives exist. One is to export a small version of the video and bring it into your animation program, forcing it to fit the window size. The results will not look that good, but it is for positioning only. Another route is to export a series of video stills, say every 10 or 20 frames, and use those as reference frames.

The two ways to composite video are rendering the animation using the video as the background, or rendering your animation without a background but creating an alpha channel with the file. Most animators prefer using the alpha channel method, called post-compositing. This allows for greater flexibility during the editing process.

When you introduce your animation file on top of a video layer in the editing program, you might want to create a shadow to enhance realism. Do this by either generating a shadow element in Photoshop and moving it over time, or using a copy of the original animation squeezing the size of the file vertically, blurring the image and using the alpha as a slightly transparent silhouette mask.

Consider applying motion blurs (see page 84) to add that final touch of realism.

COMPOSITING VIDEO AND ANIMATIONS

The important elements for success in compositing computer-generated animations on top of video is to make sure your animation lines up naturally with the video.

1

Digitize the video using a video capture board or a built-in digitizer. Capture the video using the size and frame rate you plan to use on your final product.

2

Build the model using the captured video or stills as reference for object placement. Use the video as the background image in your modeling and animation programs.

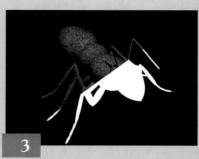

3

Render the animation using an alpha channel. Make sure the settings match the size and frame rate used when digitizing the video so it could be used as the background.

4

Bring the elements together in your editing program. You could render the animation using the captured video as a background, but bringing them together gives you more flexibility.

5

To add realism you may want to experiment with adding a slight motion blur to the object. In this case, a motion blur was applied to the back of the legs and the body of the ant using the masking tool with a blur in After Effects.

6

If your object is going to move quickly over the surface, blur the background instead, giving the effect of a panning camera. In this example, a motion blur was applied to the video layer in After Effects.

7

To keep the object from floating on the video, "ground it" by faking a shadow. To create the shadow, duplicate the animation, offset it slightly, and switch modes, using the alpha as a silhouette.

8

By changing the rotation and position of the shadow, as well as squeezing it vertically, you can give the offset shadow a more realistic feel.

9

Change the transparency of the shadow, in this case 50 percent. Experiment with ink modes. Here, a Darken mode was used.

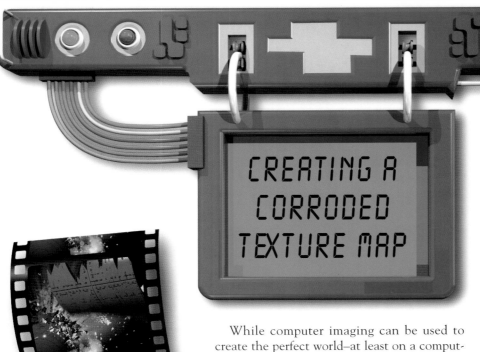

CREATING A CORRODED TEXTURE MAP

To add a more realistic surface to a model's texture, try using some of Photoshop's texture filters that ship with the program. Here, a steel plate texture has a Craquelure texture filter applied to give it more character.

While computer imaging can be used to create the perfect world–at least on a computer screen–every so often you will want a less than pristine image. Scrapes, dings, bangs, and glitches are part of the real world and can add realism. These imperfections are fairly easy to replicate in the 3D world.

Building a model with physical indentations is one way to achieve imperfection–and possibly the most realistic–yet another route exists as well. The second technique involves "abusing" the texture map, not the model. An advantage to this second method is the model is smaller in terms of polygons and will render faster. Another benefit is seen when using a corrosion effect. To alter a corrosion area, shift the position of the surface's Texture map.

Photoshop has some built-in filters that are a boon to create corrosion maps. One of the best is the Craquelure filter (found under "Filter," "Texture," "Craquelure.") You can apply this filter directly to the surface of the base texture color, but doing so alters the appearance of the original file. The best way to do this is to create a new, white layer and apply the filter to it. Since a white layer does not have anything for the filter to react with, adjust the settings for the Craquelure filter so the brightness of the cracks is lower.

Experiment with the Craquelure "crack spacing" setting. To avoid annoying repetition on a tiled texture, use a large spacing setting. If you are creating a texture map that wraps one time on an object, then you might be able to tighten up the "crack spacing" a bit. If your map is going to be "one up," you may want to go into the filtered layer with an eraser to remove some of the crack lines in selected areas.

When you have the tile you want, change the mode of the layer so the white disappears. The Multiply mode works well. The Darken mode may work, but make sure you do not lose too much detail. The final results depend on the color and darkness of the base texture and how it reacts with the filtered layer.

The real impact of the final map is from your bump map, so you do not have to run your cracked layer at 100 percent. Somewhere between 40 and 60 percent might be enough.

At this point, save the texture as an image file format that your modeling or animation program uses for importing textures.

For the corroded effect, you have to have an associated bump map to realistically give the surface a bumpy feel. You already have done most of the work. Go back to your filtered layer and change the layer settings back to a Normal mode at 100 percent. Bump maps work best when there are grey-scale edges between the whites and the blacks. To get this, soften the image by applying the Blur filter once or twice. Save the resulting file as your bump map. If your modeling program likes to have

BANGING UP A PERFECTLY GOOD MAP

If you want to roughen up a nice, clean surface, Photoshop gives you the tools to create a nice corroded feel quickly. The key is to use the onboard Craquelure filter combined with the layering tool.

1 Create the base texture. If you are going to be working with a tiling texture, remember to make it seamless. (The left, right, top, and bottom need to tile, see page 74 for details.)

2 Create a new layer and fill it with white. This is the layer where you actually create the corrosion. Do not merge it later on because we will use it again for a bump map.

3 Use the built-in Photoshop filter under Texture called Craquelure. In this example, the crack spacing was set at 100, depth at 10, and brightness at 3.

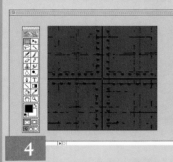

4 Change the mode of the layer with the corrosion to Multiply. Try other modes as well. Experiment with layer transparency. For this texture, 90 percent was used. Save this image as a file for texture mapping.

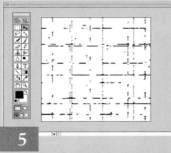

5 To make this effect work, it needs to be used with a bump map, but most of the work has been done. Go back to your corroded layer and make the mode Normal and the transparency 100 percent.

6 Apply the Blur filter to the layer twice. Bumps need gray-scale edges to work best. Save the resulting file as a gray-scale file to be used as a bump map. Some programs want this layer as an alpha channel.

the bump information in the alpha channel, copy this layer, and change it back to the earlier settings using the mode and transparency you like. Create a new alpha channel and paste the copy of the layer into the channel. Save the results as a 32-bit image.

In your modeling or animation program, treat the surface color file just like you would a regular color map. Keep in mind that the information for the bump map will be used best if the light sources are glancing lights, not straight on. Increase the settings for the bump map layer. Usually the default settings are not severe enough. Since you are creating a corrosion, you may want to get extreme and use two or three times the setting for the bump map.

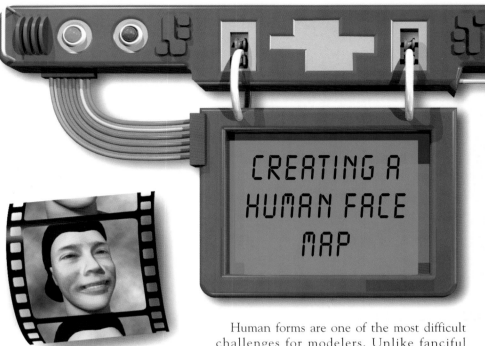

CREATING A HUMAN FACE MAP

Creating 3D humans in the computer world is difficult. Success relies on not only a good model, but a realistic surface map. The best approach to creating a quality surface map is using the model as a template for facial features placement.

Human forms are one of the most difficult challenges for modelers. Unlike fanciful spaceships and architectural designs, if a face is designed with just the oddest little accent, the anomaly quickly becomes the image's focus.

For this reason, many animators choose to buy human forms from model companies such as Viewpoint or Acuris. The model, however, presents only the first part of the challenge to creating a realistic, virtual human.

Creating texture maps for the model can be equally daunting. One solution to the challenge is tapping into the power of Photoshop's layers. After you build or buy your model, take a photo of someone who represents the texture you want to create for your model. Try to use a soft light when photographing the subject and avoid any harsh shadows. If you have a digital camera you can get right to work. Otherwise, process the film and digitize the photo either using the Kodak PhotoCD method or using your own scanner.

If your final result is for print, work on a large image that reflects the final resolution. If the final is for video, try to make the image large enough to withstand closeups. Working at twice the anticipated size generally is a good idea.

In Photoshop, edit the digitized face by removing all the hair and side details. Focus on the eyes, nose, cheeks, and mouth. Use your airbrush or feather tool to smoothly gradate the edges. With the color picker, select a color on the edge of the face and fill the edited portion with this "flesh" color.

Paste the edited photo on a new layer on top of the template. Using the Multiply mode on this layer, you should be able to see representations of both your photo and the template. Use the scale tool to push and pull your photo so it lines up with the template. Switch the photo layer back to Normal mode and export the file.

Bring the image into your modeling program and apply it to the face model. You can experiment, but the cylindrical map usually works best. Render a test image. Chances are you will need to make some adjustments. Use this initial render to make notes on changes you need to make.

Back in Photoshop make a new all "flesh"-colored layer. If you need to make a reduction, such as shrinking the mouth size, this new layer will fill in the gap left behind. Make edits by using your lasso tool with a good feather setting. Export your new edit and try out the new face.

To get everything to line up right it may take several edits. Always save your face work-file and export copies for mapping.

MAPPING A HUMAN FACE

By using a human model template and an actual photo of a person, you can create a realistic human for use in 3D animations. Here a Viewpoint head was combined with Melora's photo.

1 Most people buy a head model. A Viewpoint head is used here. If you build the head model, make sure to union all the parts into one shape.

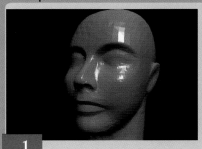

2 Set up a camera view straight on and render out the image or get a screen dump. This view serves as a template for creating the texture map.

3 Take a digital photo or scan in your subject's photograph. If possible, try to keep the lighting soft and avoid harsh shadows.

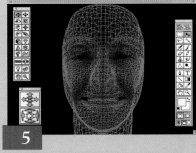

4 Edit the image in Photoshop. In this example, the left side of the subject's face was mirrored. Then everything but the main face details was edited out. Give yourself plenty of room on the sides and top.

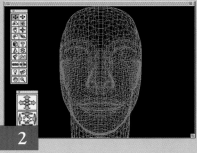

5 Using Photoshop's layers, the template was imported and a new layer created with the photo. The Multiply mode was used on this layer so both layers could be seen for positioning.

6 Chances are the template and photo are not going to line up. Use the Scale tool to reproportion the photo layer. When done, export a copy. Save the workfile for future tweaking.

7 Map the surface onto the model. A cylindrical map usually works. Render out test images to see how the alignment is working. Make notes on areas that need to be altered.

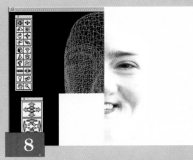

8 Go back into your workfile and tweak as needed. In this case, the mouth needed to be reduced. A new "flesh tone" layer was created under the photo.

9 Keep tweaking the image. It may take a while to get all the parts lined up. When done, create a hair model for the head.

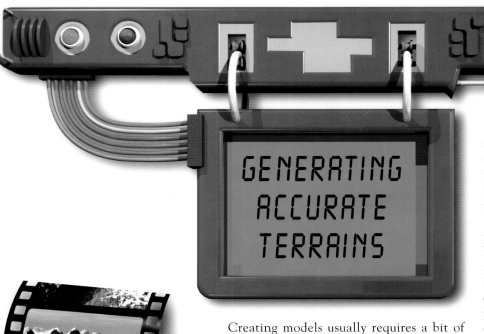

GENERATING ACCURATE TERRAINS

Scan in the area of the map you want. If the area does not have the altitudes labeled in the area you need, pencil in the information. This will be a great help for you later. Work a little larger than you need, allowing for some fudge room as you work on the project.

If your computer is connected to your scanner with Photoshop driving the scanner, you have your whole grey-scale generating studio right in front of you. If not, scan the map and bring it into Photoshop. Use the pen tool to draw along the altitude lines. Make a separate path layer for each altitude zone in which you choose to work. In our example, we drew zones every 500 feet. The final result was eight zones starting at 9,500 feet and ending at 13,000 feet. For organization purposes, the lowest zone was the lowest path.

The lightest area will be the highest areas and the darker areas will be the lowest. Create a new layer over the map template and fill it with a grey color that will leave you with all the steps you need. Set the grey by using the Hue, Saturation and Brightness settings in the Photoshop color picker. Keep the Hue and Saturation settings at 0 and adjust only the Brightness setting. A setting of 100 will be black and 0 is white. Try not to work in these extremes though. By keeping your image in the middle range, you have room for editing peaks and valleys later. Using steps of 5 or 10 on the brightness, fill each path zone on the new layer you created. When you are finished, the result should look like Step 4 on the next page.

To add in details such as mountain peaks, crevices and pockets, use the Dodge and Burn tools. Use the Gaussian blur filter on the entire layer. Set the blur high enough to remove any of the zone edges. If the edges are even slightly apparent, a stair-stepping effect will result. For our example, a blur of 30 pixels was used. If any important details are lost in the blur, use the Dodge and Burn tools to clean the image up.

Bring the grey-scale image into your modeling program and work with it like you would any object, applying textures and scaling it so the vertical height reflects the true scale of the area.

If you are interested in terrains with a more global perspective, you can map the "Globe" texture map (included on the CD-ROM) onto a sphere or use one of Digital Wisdom's Mountain High Maps for high resolution, crisp mapping.

Photoshop can be a powerhouse for interpreting map data into an accurate grey-scale image for creating 3D terrain models. The image below of the mountains around Telluride was created using a map of the area, a scanner, Photoshop, and Bryce.

Creating models usually requires a bit of artistic deft-of-hand and the skills of a talented modeler to create a good looking object. And then every so often a project comes along when all the data is handed to you and it is as straightforward as drawing in a coloring book. Creating 3D maps from topographical data is an example of one of those animals. All that is needed is a scanner, Photoshop, a modeling program that imports grey-scale data for terrains, and a lot of patience.

Most large cities have map stores that are wealthy resources of topographical information. If you do not have a map store near you, visit the United States Geographical Survey at www.usgs.gov. The Survey can supply you with a map of almost every area in the world.

CREATING AN ACCURATE TERRAIN

Photoshop provides all the tools necessary to create an accurate grey-scale map from topographical data. Most modeling and landscape generation programs allow for the import of grey-scale images to create terrains.

1
Find a map of the area you want to create. Make sure the altitudes are clearly labeled. If not, make the task easier by writing in the altitudes.

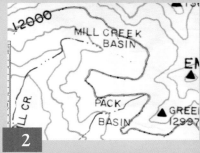

2
If you did not use the Acquire plug-in driver, import the scan into Photoshop. Use the pen tool to trace the altitude lines. In this example we drew new zones for every 500 feet.

3
Fill each zone with a different grey shade. Using the Hue, Saturation, and Brightness (HSB) settings, keep the hue and saturation at 0. Change the brightness in increments of 10.

4
Mountain peaks and small pockets can be numerous and do not quite make the next step for their own zone. Use the Dodge tool for mountain peaks and the Burn tool for pockets.

5
Use the Gaussian blur tool on the scene. With enough blur, no zone edges can be seen (avoid stair-stepping effect). Fix any lost detail using the Dodge and Burn tools.

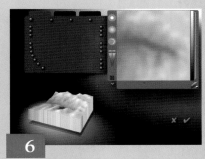

6
Export your grey-scale file and bring it into your modeling program. In this case, it was imported into Bryce. Most modeling programs allow for the import of grey-scale data.

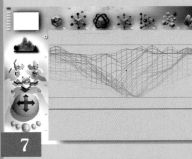

7
The scale you created in Photoshop may be too extreme or too shallow when the model is generated. View the model from the side and scale the shape vertically until it reflects the actual height.

8
If you want an accurate terrain, create it from scratch in Photoshop using your grey-scale work file as a template or use procedural texture generators like the one in Bryce.

9
The final result is rendered and is output as a file for compositing in a final animation or is an integral part of the final scene.

BUILDING A 3D FOREST

Building a tree leaf by leaf would be a task even the best model builder would dread. Thanks to products like Tree Professional, most of the work can be handed over to your computer. The tree below was created in Tree Professional in less than five minutes by simply filling in a few tree variables, such as trunk width and leaf type. The final result was saved as a .dxf file and brought into Electric Image for rendering, about five minutes in this example.

A few tricks and products are available to keep you from building a tree leaf by leaf. Modelers can choose between three general directions for building trees.

Building a handful of leaves and duplicating them (or using instancing, if available) onto modeled trunks and branches is the traditional route. While you have complete control over the outcome, the process is daunting. This difficult route gives you the kind of detail you need if your camera is going to be extremely close to the tree.

A second method is to buy a tree-generating program like Onyx's Tree Professional. Incredibly accurate trees can be generated by inputting desired variables on the tree's specifications, such as leaf type, foliage color, trunk width, and base design. To get realistic trees with little work, this is definitely the way to go. The program quickly pays for itself when compared to the time it takes to make a single tree with traditional modeling. The only down side is the final size of the trees. If you are designing a model of a building and you want to put a tree in the front yard, use it. If you are designing a golf course and you are dealing with hundreds of trees, this way will kill you.

A third option is to design faux trees that resemble trees, but if you look closely, they are just flat planks with tree surfaces mapped to them. Obviously, you would not do this if your camera was going to get too close to the tree. But, if you are populating a horizon or background with trees, this may be your answer.

To design faux trees, you need to create your 2D tree outline that will become your tree plank. Avoid drawing half the tree and mirror imaging the other half. This would be too symmetrical. Draw the shape with a rough edge that gives you the feel of an overhanging branch.

When you have finished your shape, map a texture of tree leaves on the top. To get the leaf texture, take a photo of a tree or use the tree image found on the CD-ROM that comes with this book. After mapping the surface color on your plank, replicate and rotate the tree plank on its center axis–depending on the tree you could do this once or twice. Go back into the new tree planks and edit them to give the tree planks a slightly different feel. Shift around some of the branches to keep a pattern from developing.

Monitor what your lights are doing. If you are planning to render with shadows, you may find harsh shadows being created on the planks. To avoid this you can: 1) keep the main light close to the camera; 2) use a strong fill light; 3) turn off shadows on the tree planks or; 4) raise the ambient light.

If you are planning a quick camera sweep or

MAKING A FAUX TREE

If you need a tree for background noise in a scene, you may not want to deal with the thousands of polygons that can go into creating even a small tree. One shortcut is creating a tree from a multi-faceted 2D shape, resulting in fast renders and reasonable trees.

1 Create an extruded object with the general outline of the tree. Make rough edges and avoid using a mirror tool to replicate sides.

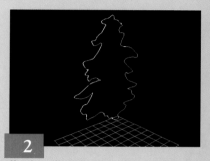

2 Use the outline to create a flat, extruded shape. Squeeze the shape of the tree as thin as possible so the edge of the shape is barely visible.

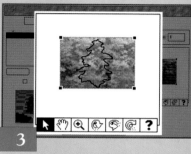

3 Map a tree leaf surface onto the shape. You can take a picture of a real tree or use the tree texture included on the CD-ROM.

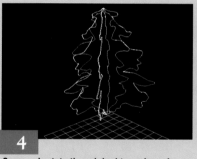

4 Copy and rotate the original tree shape from the center of the tree. You can make as many duplicates as you want, but usually two or three will work. If your trees will be in the distance and not very noticeable, a tree form with just two shapes in an "X" work fine.

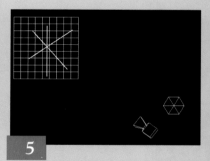

5 Adjust your light position. You may find that a light closer to the camera keeps harsh shadows to a minimum. You also may want to experiment with fill lights. Bringing up the ambient light helps.

6 The final tree may not be anything you want to get your camera close to, but if you are building a forest, this technique helps keep down the rendering time.

using these trees in clumps in the background, you will find that they work well. If you need a forest with hundreds of trees, this technique works great and you can simply copy the tree plank outline to keep the overall polygon count within reason.

If you are more concerned with polygon count instead of rendering time, you may want to experiment with creating simple forms, possibly even spheres, with a noise-generated transparency map that pokes holes through a green object, giving a general full-formed tree feel. A few of these transparency-mapped trees can trounce you on rendering time, but will give you true 3D trees with a low polygon count.

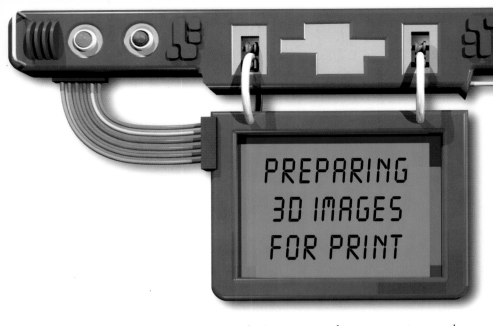

PREPARING 3D IMAGES FOR PRINT

A time comes when most animators have to translate images to the print world. Even if you have no desire for doing print illustration, there is a good chance someone will want some of your image files for promotional work and packaging.

Most animations are produced at a screen resolution of 72 dpi. Unless you plan on using your images at a postage-stamp size in print, you will have to output at a higher resolution for better quality. While a screen image looks fine at 72 dpi on your monitor, it looks like hash when printed out full size.

To work around this, increase the size of your image. Some programs go as far as to let

The image below was created using standard 3D animation tools, but was output at a high resolution for print reproduction. Key factors to keep in mind were the gamma settings and the resolution of the textures used in the scene.

you type in the inches and resolution you want, but others only let you set your output size. This is where it can get tricky. To determine your output resolution, you can use our handy-dandy image resolution chart on the next page. Your final resolution will be based on two variables: the size you want the image and the dpi you want the final output to be.

To figure your dpi, find out what your printer or imagesetter wants. The range usually bounces around 200 to 300 dpi. After you find the magic number, follow the instructions on the chart to determine the resolution you will need to output your work. For instance, to get a 3-inch wide by 4-inch tall image to look good at 300 dpi, set your final render size to be 898 points by 1198 points. If your numbers do not fall squarely with the numbers in the chart (if you need a 3.5-inch image at 260 dpi), the route to follow to devise your own formula also is outlined.

Print images run quite a bit darker than video images, so it is a good idea to either boost up the lighting in your scene before you render it or open the file in Photoshop and tweak the curves. In general, you can boost the lighting of an image by going to the curves setting. Find the line's centerpoint. Moving to the left, find the square grid box. In this grid box, click in the center. This automatically adjusts the lighting. The curve (at right) depicts the way the line looks after this adjustment. Make sure your image is still in the RGB mode before you make this adjustment.

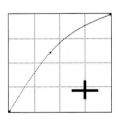

Most printers like images to be saved as CMYK files. You will notice the image muddies up a bit when you change to this mode, but do not worry. The final image will most likely print more saturated than what you see on your screen.

Different imagesetters and printers like different formats. For print work, you will most likely be saving as Encapsulated Postscript (EPS) or Tagged Image File Format (TIFF or TIF), both of which import easily into most page layout programs.

SIZING UP AN IMAGER

Some rendering programs allow direct input of inches and dpi settings, some do not. If you need to render an image for print work and the only output setting you have is for the size of the image, render the scene larger to fit the final output. The chart below covers image sizes in inch increments. If you need an odd size, multiply your inches by 72 to get the point width of the image. Then multiply that number by the dpi multiplier shown below. For instance, if you have an image that will be 8.5-inches wide, multiply 8.5 by 72 to get your image's point width (612 points). If you are planning to render the image for a magazine and they want 220 dpi images, multiply your pixel width of 612 by the dpi multiplier, 3.05, to get the final width of your render output (1867). Follow the same formula for the image's height. After you have rendered the scene you can open the render in Photoshop and change the dpi setting from 72 to 220. With the Resample Image button unchecked, you will see your width change from 25.9 inches to 8.5 and your height will follow (assuming the size also is proportionately checked).

		Resolution		
Inches	Points	160 dpi (newsprint)	220 dpi (magazine)	300 dpi (books, posters)
		Multiplier 2.22	3.05	4.16
1	72	160	220	299
2	144	320	439	599
3	216	479	659	898
4	288	639	878	1198
5	360	799	1098	1498
6	432	959	1318	1797
7	504	1119	1537	2097
8	576	1279	1757	2396
9	648	1439	1976	2696
10	720	1598	2196	2995
11	792	1758	2416	3295
12	864	1918	2635	3594

To figure out a formula for a dpi not listed above, take the dpi you will need and divide by 72. For example, if you need a 260 dpi image, take 260, divide by 72, and get 3.61. By multiplying the pixel width of your image by the new dpi multiplier, you will get your proper rendering width.

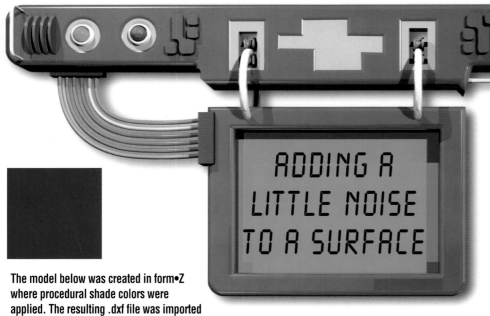

ADDING A LITTLE NOISE TO A SURFACE

The model below was created in form•Z where procedural shade colors were applied. The resulting .dxf file was imported into Electric Image for rendering with many of the same procedural colors still used. The manipulator arms, pontoons, and craft frames were covered with a simple noise texture (above) to keep from being plastic-like. The seafloor also was covered with an embossed noise texture map.

A good model can be killed by bad surfacing and sometimes the worst job that can be done on an object's texture is not to apply a surface at all. When dealing with a complex object with dozens or even hundreds of parts, it is easy to apply a procedural surface color by default and continue to focus on the detail of

an object. While applying procedural colors to an object is certainly the quickest route, it is also the quickest way to render your image unrealistic–unless your object is made out of plastic. Even complex shaders such as marbles and woods tend to have a flat, glossy look about them. To avoid these pitfalls, apply texture maps to even seemingly insignificant parts. If the object you are dealing with does not have a lot of drama to start with, like a painted wall or a desktop, you will do better if you take the time to create a texture map to apply to the surface of the object.

In the scenes below, hundreds of mechanical objects, wires, pipes, tubes, rivets, and cables combine to make the final scene. While the object has its share of procedural colors, the main objects, even ones with flat colors, have texture maps applied. The two orange pontoons, seafloor, blue frame, and skids, for instance, were rendered with a simple texture map.

For the seafloor, a brown field was created with a noise applied. Since Photoshop's Noise filter tends to make a grainy, multi-colored noise, the resulting image was altered in the color balance to add more yellow. Then the whole object was enlarged 300 percent. Then this file was blurred and the Gallery Effects Emboss filter (which ships with Photoshop)

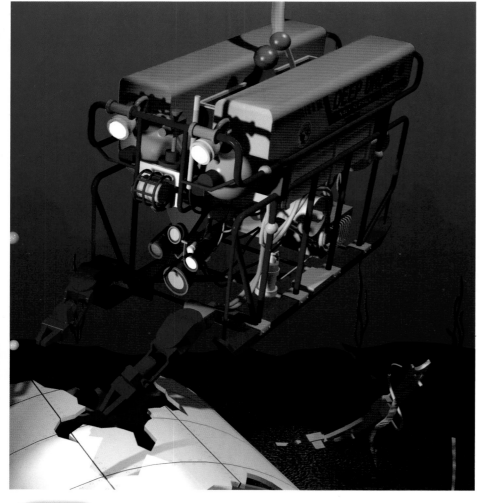

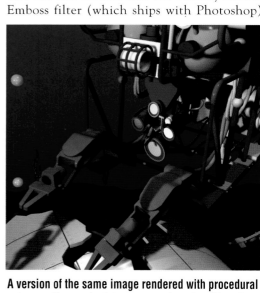

A version of the same image rendered with procedural colors on the manipulator arms and on the side rails shows the importance of even simple texture maps. Without the texture maps, the objects loose their "tooth" and seem to be made out of plastic.

CREATING NOISE TEXTURES

The seafloor texture in the scene on the left hand page was generated completely in Photoshop using standard noise and emboss tools. The embossed feel was emphasized by using the same image information for the bump map.

1

Create the color field that reflects the general color of the final surface.

2

Use Photoshop's built-in Noise filter. Adjust the noise to suit you. The higher the setting, the more contrast in the noise. A setting of 10 was used here.

3

The Noise filter creates a multi-colored grain, so adjust the color balance and hue settings to bring your color range back to where you need it.

4

If the grain is too tight for your use, simply enlarge the document size or scale it by hand. To enlarge the above image, the upper left-hand quarter was selected and scaled to fill the document size.

5

Using the Gallery Effects Emboss filter, apply an emboss to the image. Manipulate the settings to get the desired height. Here a height setting of 8 was used. Blur or despeckle the surface to remove unwanted noise.

6

To get a real bumpy surface, make a bump map. Convert a copy of your surface color to grey-scale and use it as the bump map when compositing your surface texture.

was applied. To accent the bumpiness, a copy of this file was turned into a grey-scale file and used as a bump map.

To keep the blue frame from looking like it was made from plastic, a small blue field was created in Photoshop and a slight noise of 10 pixels was applied. The resulting file then was cubically mapped to the object. For the orange pontoons, a small orange square was created from the same color that would be used on the decal map and applied cubically to the entire object.

To see the contrast between a procedural shade and a texture map on the same object, a close-up version of the deep-sea robot was made using procedural shades on the side rails and the manipulator arms (previous page, lower right). Without the simple texture map the object flattens out and looks more like plastic than metal. The end result is an object that looks more like a toy than a realistic deep-sea drone.

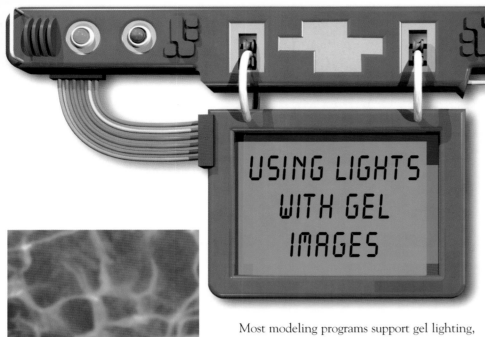

USING LIGHTS WITH GEL IMAGES

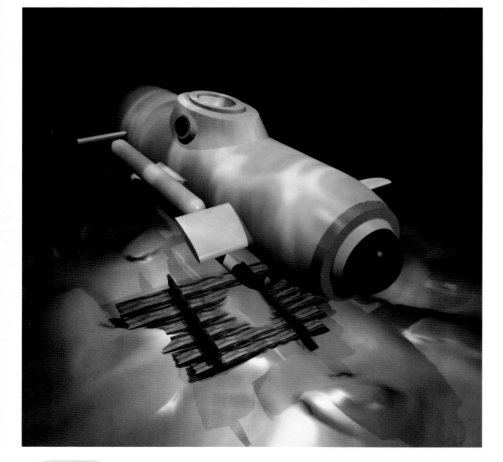

The Wraptures pool texture, above, was used in the scene below as a gel light source. A 15-degree outer cone angle was used on the scene, with a 10-degree inner cone to feather the edge of the light softly.

Most modeling programs support gel lighting, but it is often a feature that remains quietly in the background, forgotten and unused. Using gel lighting is not as mystical or difficult as many assume and could be used to add important accent lighting to most scenes.

Gels, image files that can be projected from a source light, usually can be attached to spotlights and the area of the outer cone is usually the area used by the gel. With this in mind, you have to keep the size of your image proportionate to the area that you want to illuminate with the gel.

As an example, the water gel image used on the submersible scene was 400 pixels wide. To get it to work properly on the sub, a cone angle of 15 degrees was used with the light source not too far above the all-white craft. If a wider cone angle was used, say around 50 degrees, only a small portion of the water reflection detail would be seen and the sub would be mostly a solid blue color. If you want to cover a large area but your image file is not big enough, tile your image on a larger canvas size. For instance, if the water color was needed over a larger area, the seamless texture from Wraptures could be selected in Photoshop, made into a pattern, and a larger new document would be created and filled with the pattern.

It is important to use a fill light when working with gels. If your only light source is the gel light, the shadows will be harsh and the scene unrealistic. One or two fill lights help round out the scene and allow the gel light to become an accent element instead of a dominant element. Keep in mind that the color on your gel is going to influence the color of everything within the gel light area. If you have a nice yellow area and you are using a gel light with lots of blue, then you are bound to end up with a greenish tint.

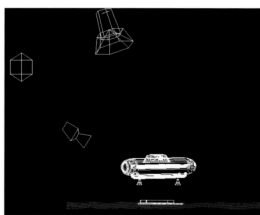

A typical scene using a gel light shows the spotlight, on top, with the gel attached. In this case, an outer cone of 15 degrees was used. A fill light on the left helped even out the overall lighting, and two accent lights can be seen underneath the sub.

CHAPTER FOUR

WHEN THE DUST SETTLES...

If there is only one thing you learn in the process of writing a book, it is that nobody is right. As much as we would like to think there is a knighted caste of animators who rule supreme, the rules keep changing and when the dust settles, everyone is playing catch-up to the latest technology shift. All you can count on, after a while, is raw talent.

Beginning my art career in the early '80s, I often heard the phrase "...why I've been doing this for over 30 years and..." and the classic "...because that's the way we've always done it." Computers turned these phrases upside down. The last thing a person would say in the computer industry is, "I've been using the same program for five years, so don't you go telling me how to do my job." In an industry where most companies are pledged to turn out a new version of their program every six months, clinging onto old habits will quickly leave you in the dust.

As much as we would like to think that the "raw talent" factor will keep most of us ahead of the curve, the reality is both new tools and developing talent enhance each other. In some cases, the single ability to work faster will spur on more creativity. In other cases, previously unavailable features will give artists new tools to experiment and with which they will evolve as artists. It is a continual and exhausting process.

Which programs are the best? Which platforms are the best? Log on to any on-line message board and ask these questions and you start a virtual war that lasts for weeks. Everyone likes to think that after they made an investment in a platform and spent a bundle on software, they made the right choice. Tell them they did not, and the fur starts flying. It is human nature to defend one's decisions and the answer to the questions are not easy.

After the publication of our first book, *Animation and 3D Modeling on the Mac*, the most frequently asked question e-mailed to us was, "What software should I buy?" Not only is

Co-author Don Foley uses a variety of 3D tools to get through the day. As a freelance illustrator, the variety of assignments crossing his desk require an equal variety in the tools used to tackle the projects. Tapping into both the strengths of the Mac and the Windows platforms, he has found that the world is moving away from platform dependency. When the dust settles, he prefers watercolors, which are generally platform independent. Feel free to stop by and visit at www.foley-media.com

the choice a serious investment for most people, it often defines their abilities and growth for the future. In this one-on-one forum, we could find out what the particular needs of the individual were and make a suggestion or two. In writing a book, it is not so easy.

While it would be a simple matter to skirt around the issue and not tick-off the software publishers who produce some really good programs, it also would be a disservice to many readers who buy books looking for answers.

The compromise is to make some suggestions and bury them in the back of the book, in sort of a "this is our opinion, not the gospel."

For starters, platforms aside, chances are you already own a computer and know what you want to do with it. So, even though we lean toward the Mac side of the spectrum, the reality is that the bulk of the animators are Windows users. Fortunately, most programs are available on both platforms and give equal quality results cross-platform. So do not expect us to even get close to that fray. It is too emotional.

If you are starting off in animation and have a limited budget, both Infini-D and StudioPro offer solid results with little investment. We often recommend these programs to students, not only because they are reasonably priced, but also because you can really do some great work with them, depending on the effort you give to mastering the programs. We also recommend these programs to studios whose focus in not animation but who need the occasional 3D element for whatever reason. Both are easy to learn and can play an important role in a studio environment without taxing time or resources too much.

We used to carve out a section for middle-of-the-road users, but this demographic hardly exists any more. Either you do a lot of 3D and animation work or you do not. The price range of most high-end programs has dropped to where the middle range programs used to be, with a few exceptions such as Softimage.

If 3D is your life, then you will want a tool that can respond to your needs. Windows users can find this in 3D Studio Max. Mac users can find it in Electric Image. In addition to these two programs, form•Z, a CAD-esque modeling program, is a complex but important tool that offers incredible modeling capability.

So where does this leave all the other programs? It does not leave them anywhere. These choices are personal opinion, but we have a huge amount of respect for all the programs and discourage program-based elitism that is prevalent in the on-line world. We have seen great things done in trueSpace, Designer, Extreme 3D, and Lightwave, among others.

The support programs are also key and should be considered as important as picking a modeler. You have to have Photoshop. You should have Poser. Detailer is a solid tool. Kai's Power Tools are important. After Effects is the best in animation editing and element motion control. Bryce is a good tool to have around, so is Tree Professional. For video editing either Speed Razor for Windows or Premiere for the Mac will take care of you. If you do multimedia work, we prefer Director for authoring and tools like Eye Candy for futzing with objects. If you are doing serious landscaping, nothing beats World Construction Set. For sound editing, Sound Forge is our Windows preference while SoundEdit 16, with Deck II for mixing, is our Mac preference.

Several resources help meet deadlines. We keep Digital Wisdom's Mountain High Maps on hand for land surfaces and globes, Artbeats' City Surfaces and Interiors for quick buildings, and Artbeats' Fire and Explosion clips for blowing things up. Wraptures I and II disks are invaluable texture sources, as are Pixar's Classic and 128 textures. People tell us that Infographica is one of the best sources for models, as well as Viewpoint and Acuris. For general sound effects, you cannot beat Sound Idea's "The General" package.

A few years ago the only place to go for serious animation was an SGI workstation. Things are changing quickly and studios are turning more to Windows and Mac to create professional animations. The result is a fantastic rush from 3D companies to improve their products to match SGI standards and for companies publishing programs for the SGI to bring down costs to fend off the competition. This creates a favorable environment for an industry that hardly existed five years ago and is now sweeping the globe.

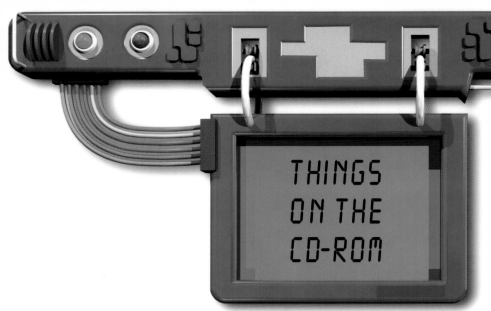

DXF MODELS

Booster
Blood cells
Gravel Car
GOES Satellite
Lear Jet
Parking meter
Mosquito
Pistons
Shakers
Shuttle
Stealth Bomber
Train
Yacht

Plus 12 Acuris models!

SOUND FILES

Angels	Machine
Bells	Music 1
Cymbal	Music 2
Drum 1	Ship hum 1
Drum 2	Ship hum 2
Fanfare	Slideshow
Gentle	Sparkle
Gunshot	Sparkle 2
Harmony	Synvibe
Helicopter	Synthsong
Floating	Techvibe
Highlite	

As a general rule, animators never have enough textures, sound effects, models, or backgrounds. The CD-ROM with this book is designed to give you some tools you can use in the creation of your animations.

One texture alone–Globe–is worth the price of the book. Globe was created using a compilation of NASA photos available to the public. The images were edited, retouched, and designed to act as a high-resolution spherical map of the Earth.

The textures are saved in TARGA (.tga) format for Windows and PICT format for the Macintosh. Sound files are saved as AIFF (.aif) files for Windows and Macintosh. Model files are in DXF format, which imports into all known modeling programs regardless of platform. Backgrounds are 640x480 pixels.

Also on the disk is a Guide that serves as an interactive catalog. The CD-ROM Guide gives viewers samples of the textures, sounds, models, and backgrounds. A slideshow of selected images from the book and an animation clip compiled from a variety of animators are included.

The textures, sound effects, models, and backgrounds on the CD-ROM are yours to use in your animations, royalty free. For instance, you can map the globe surface onto a sphere, animate the globe by rotating it, and sell the final result to a client. But you cannot sell the globe texture.

Other textures can be found at our Web site in JPEG format.

TEXTURES

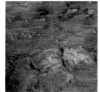

Bedrock
seamless stone

Block
seamless block

Building
modern facade

Bulkhead
steel wall

CD-ROM
gold disk

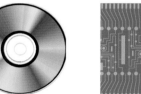

Circuit
computer board

Concrete
seamless texture

Corroded
rusted metal

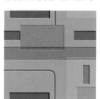

Craft
spacecraft

Dirt
rocky earth

Dollar
generic bill

Duct
galvanized steel

Facade
modern facade

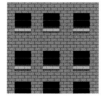

Facade2
apartments

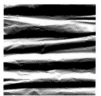

Foil
aluminum wrap

Globe
complete earth

Granite
rough stone

Land
terrain surface

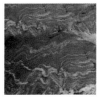

Marble
smooth stone

Moss
grassy moss

Ocean
sea texture

Old wall
grody brick

Orinside
orange insides...

Orskin
...bumpy outsides

Page
desk clutter tile

Plank
good for floors

Rivet
welded sheets

Roadcut
road cutaway

Sidewalk
polished surface

Slate
smooth stone

Soccer
tiled ball surface

Tile
ceramic tile

Toxic
steel drum wrap

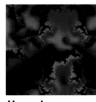

Vein
organic tile

Vessel
blood vessels

Walkway
subway wall

BACKGROUNDS

Clouds
nice day

Curtain
stage setting

Dunes
bumpy terrain

Earth
globe backdrop

Fractal
fractal lightning

Map
old map

Organic
mottled shapes

Screen
CD background

Scrub
desert scrub

Seal
U.S. president

Stars
starry night

Trees
leaf foliage

ARTISTS FROM
THE GALLERY

The work from the artist's gallery section of the book is done by a wide range of 3D artists, a quirky combination of old friends, old co-workers, artists who had their work in our first book, new friends, and people we have never met before who answered postings put on various on-line bulletin boards. Their response was great. We feel very honored that they have shared their work with us and the 3D/animation community. Their work expresses the visions that can be created using the tools at hand.

A good portion of these artists started using 3D in its early stages. It has been a joy watching their work, as well as that of the entire 3D industry, improve and evolve every year. The evolution has not been one-sided with just the companies releasing new versions because it is a nice thing to do–these artists and others around the world have demanded the growth, always pushing new tools and features to their limits, and paving the way for future applications.

Most of these artists are freelancers, working out of their offices, basements and spare bedrooms. They have tapped into a common thread of visualization that allows them to create previously unvisited worlds, the realms of their imaginations, using low cost computing systems that show others that you do not have to have an SGI to rule. They are, in their own right, visionaries. Following is a contact listing for most of the animators and illustrators. This is provided as a service for you, if you ever need freelance illustrators and animators, and as a service to them for providing their images for this book.

BILL BAKER
pages 21,22
9338 South Whitt Drive
Manassas Park, VA 20111
703 330-2843

TROY BENESCH
pages 17, 20, 23
Videoactv Studios
1487 Chain Bridge Road
Suite #105
McLean, VA 22101
703 760-0440

KEVIN CAHILL
pages 26, 28
Asco
New York, NY 10010
212 260-2511
Digitect@Earthlink.net

KEITH CARTER
pages 23, 26
2416 K Street NW
Suite 606
Washington, D.C. 20037
202 467-6829

MARILYNN DESILVA
page 34
SeeScape
28110 Poppy Drive
Willits, CA 95490
707 459-3194
marilynn@zapcom.net

SHARKAWI CHE DIN
pages 22, 24, 28
609 Abercorn Street 2E
Savannah, GA 31401
912 231-8792
sharkawi@earthlink.com

JOHN FINDLEY

pages 21, 34
500 Stanyan Street
San Francisco, CA 94117
sweaz@aol.com

DON FOLEY

pages 19, 20, 25, 26, 29
www.foleymedia.com
don@foleymedia.com
703 849-1707

SHELLY GREEN

pages 23, 30, 31, 34
45 Marimar Street
Thousand Oaks, CA 91360
shetland@west.net
www.west.net~shetland

FRANK KANACH

pages 30, 32, 33, 34
301 230-9482
swivel@nicom.com

PETER KOHAMA

pages 20, 22, 24, 28, 30
1600 S. Eads St. #209-N
Arlington, VA 22202
xanadux@pop.dn.net

DENNIS LOWE

pages 17, 18, 21, 23
6011 North 19th Road
Arlington, VA 22205
703 533-3474

FRANK MCINTYRE

page 33
Pixel Workshop, Inc.
9650 Santiago Road
Suite 3
Columbia MD 21045
410 715-9050
frank@pixelworkshop.com

GREG NEVIUS

pages 17, 18, 27
animationISTATION
1204 LeGrande Street
Suite 3
Berwick, PA 18603
717 759-3738 (phone & fax)
gnevius@geocities.com

E.W. PARRIS

page 23
ewparris studios
Centreville,VA
ewparris@aol.com

AMY SAMELSON

page 24, 26-27
Asco
New York, N.Y. 10010
212 260-2511
Digitect@Earthlink.net

ROBERT SHARO

pages 17, 21, 22, 24, 26, 28
Infinity Multimedia
1005 Surrey Woods Road
Bethel Park ,PA
412 831-3095
infinity@nb.net

KEVIN SHAWLEY

page 16
Orbital Sciences Corporation
shawley.kevin@orbital.com

JUAN THOMASSIE

pages 18, 27
5705 North 15th Road
Arlington VA 22205
703 532-4254
jmt@nicom.com

HANS WESTMAN

page 21
429 W. 11th Street
Claremont, CA 91711
909 621-1088
hans@tstonramp.com

MICHELLE WILSON

page 28
Asco
New York, NY 10010
212-260-2511
Digitect@Earthlink.net

AGATA WOJACZEK

pages 27, 30, 31, 32
Advanced Graphics Applications
2200 Sherobee Rd.
Suite 702
Mississauga, Ontario, Canada
L5A-3Y3
905-306-1020
agand@clo.com
www.clo.com/~agand

ANDRZEJ WOJACZEK

pages 27, 30, 31, 32
Advanced Graphics Applications
2200 Sherobee Road
Suite 702
Mississauga, Ontario, Canada
L5A-3Y3
905 306-1020
agand@clo.com
www.clo.com/~agand

COMPANIES
MAKING IT
POSSIBLE

It is an incredibly fast-paced race to produce the best 3D package with the most features and to sell it at the most reasonable price. The clear winner is us, the users. The competition between companies creating products for the 3D world is hot. The result is a fantastic toolbox for the users. Weaker products get weeded out quickly and strong feature sets are generally rewarded by being copied by all the competitors. But the race goes on. We are glad it does.

We have a great amount of respect for all the companies in the 3D marketplace. They have given us the tools to realize our dreams. The prices have been set so anyone from hobbyists to professionals can access the programs. If you consider what the market looked like in the late 1980's compared to now, you realize that they were not building on tried-and-true methods and just charging ahead with blatant capitalism. They were carving a path through a technological wilderness and their programmers were working blind. Many of the concepts and developments that were being explored did not build on existing technology. They were forged in the heat of the moment to solve a problem that had never existed before. A very impressive feat.

The result is not one or two major players, but dozens of high-quality 3D animation packages handling tasks from creating textures, building models, rendering, and editing the final compositions. When asked to participate in this book, almost all of the companies approached dove in and gave us a hand. We would like to thank them for their support. A thriving 3D community exists because of their efforts and vision.

ACURIS, INC.

Acuris Models

1098 Washington Crossing Road
Suite 2
Washington Crossing, PA 18977
800 652-2874

A useful set of human figures along with a wide selection of models.

ADOBE

After Effects
Illustrator
Photoshop
Premiere

P.O. Box 7900
Mountain View, CA 94039
800 447-3577

High-quality multimedia products with great manuals and tutorials.

ALIAS RESEARCH INC.

Sketch!

110 Richmond Street East
Toronto, Ontario, Canada
M5C1P1
416 362-9181

A good modeling and still image rendering program.

ALIEN SKIN SOFTWARE

Eye Candy

800 St. Mary's Street
Raleigh, NC 27605
919 832-4124

A Photoshop plug-in that saves time creating some cool and often-used effects.

ARTBEATS SOFTWARE, INC.

City Surface
Interiors
ReelExplosions 1 and 2
ReelFire 1 and 2

P.O. Box 709
Myrtle Creek, OR 97457
541 863-4429
www.artbeats.com

A great resource for construction textures and generic backgrounds. The fire and explosion CDs are in QuickTime and Targa D1 formats.

AUTO-DES-SYS

form•Z

2011 Riverside Drive
Columbus, OH 43221
614 488-8838

A world class modeling program.

BYTE BY BYTE CORP.

Sculpt 3D

39225 West Baker Lane
Suite 3229
Austin, TX
512 305-0360

A good modeling and still-image rendering program.

CALIGARI CORP.

trueSpace

1959 Landings Drive
Mountain View, CA 94043
415 390-9600

A Windows-based modeling, animation, and rendering program.

DATA TRANSLATION

Media 100

503 460-1600

A non-linear editing system.

DIGIMATION

Studio Max plug-ins

www.digimation.com
800 854-4496

An impressive collection of plug-ins.

DIGITAL PROCESSING SYSTEMS

Perception Video

606 371-5533
www.dps.com

A landscape and terrain program.

DIGITAL WISDOM, INC.

Mountain High Maps

P.O. Box 2070
Tappahannock, VA 22560-2070
804 758-0670

Earth images for texture maps.

ELECTRIC IMAGE

Electric Image Animation System
Electric Image Modeler

117 E. Colorado Boulevard
Suite 300
Pasadena, CA 91105

Powerful animation and modeling for Windows and Mac.

EQUILIBRIUM

DeBabelizer

475 Gate Five Road
Suite 225
Sausalito, CA 94965
800 534-8651

A must-have translator and batch processing tool.

FORM & FUNCTION

Wraptures

1595 17th Avenue
San Francisco, CA 94122
415 664-4010

A reasonably priced set of must-have tiled textures and assorted backgrounds.

HASH, INC.

Animation Master

2800 East Evergreen Boulevard
Vancouver, WA 98611
206 750-0042

A Photoshop plug-in for creating 3D terrain meshes.

IN:SYNC

Speed Razor

301 320-0220
www.in-sync.com

A video editing program for Windows.

KINETIX

Studio Max

111 McInnis Parkway
San Rafael, CA 94903
800 879-4233

A world-class animation program.

KNOLL SOFTWARE

CyberMesh

P.O. Box 6887
San Rafael, CA 94903
415 453-2471

A Photoshop plug-in for creating 3D terrain meshes.

LIGHTSCAPE TECHNOLOGY

Lightscape Visualization System

408 246-1155
www.lightscape.com

Architectural modeling for Windows NT.

MACROMEDIA

Deck II
Director
Extreme 3D
FreeHand
SoundEdit
xRes

600 Townsend Street
Suite 408
San Francisco, CA 94103
415 252-2000

A whole suite of tools for creation and production.

METACREATIONS

Bryce
Detailer
Final Effects
Infini-D
Kai's Power Tools
KPT Convolver
Painter
Poser
Ray Dream Designer

6303 Carpinteria Avenue
Carpinteria, CA 93013
805 566-6200

A company that has absorbed a lot of good programs. Their product list is almost a must-have list for great supporting animation and effects programs.

MICROSOFT

Softimage

www.microsoft.com
818 365-1359

A powerful Windows NT animation program.

MIDISOFT

Studio

1605 N.W. Sammamish Road
Suite 205
Issaquah, WA 98027
206 391-3610

Windows MIDI editing program.

NEWTEK

Lightwave 3D

1200 S.W. Executive Drive
Topeka, KS 66615
913 288-8000

A modeling, animation, and rendering program for both Windows and Mac.

NORTHERN LIGHTS

Dante
Pathfinder
Zeus

310 376-4266

Electric Image plug-ins.

ONYX COMPUTING

Tree Professional

10 Avon Street
Cambridge, MA 02138
617 876-3876

A must-have program if you plan on including trees in your animations.

OPCODE SYSTEMS, INC.

MusicShop
Vision

3950 Fabian Way
Suite 100
Palo Alto, CA 94303
415 856-3333

Mac MIDI editing program.

PIXAR

Classic Textures
128

1001 West Cutting
Richmond, CA 94804
510 236-4000

A seamless texture collection.

QUESTAR PRODUCTIONS

World Construction Set

1058 Weld County Road 235
Brighton, CO 80601
303 659-4028

A great landscape and terrain modeling and rendering tool for Windows and Mac.

SONIC FOUNDRY

Sound Forge

100 South Baldwin
Suite 204
Madison, WI 53703
608 256-3133

A solid sound editing program for Windows 95 and Windows NT.

SOUND IDEAS

The General

105 West Beaver Creek Road
Suite 4
Richmond Hill, Ontario, Canada
L4B1C6
800 387-3030

Pre-recorded audio and sound effects.

STRATA

Media Paint
StudioPro

2 West Saint George Boulevard
Suite 2100
St. George, UT 84770
800 787-2823

A solid all-around modeling and animatic system for Windows and Mac.

TERRAN INTERACTIVE

Movie Cleaner Pro

2 North First Street
San Jose, CA 95113
800 577-3443

A QuickTime movie compression utility.

THE VALIS GROUP

Pixel Putty
Cookie Cutter and Tenderizer

2270 Paradise Drive
Tiburon, CA 94920
415 435-5404

A 3D animation program and Electric Image plug-ins.

VIEWPOINT DATA LABS

Bunches and Bunches of models

625 S. State Street
Orem, UT 84058
800 DATA-SET

A fantastic resource for difficult- or impossible-to-build models.

VISUAL CONCEPTS ENGINEERING

Pyromania I
Pyromania II

13300 Ralston Avenue
Sylmar, CA 91342
818 367-9187

Flames, Explosions, Sparks, and Smoke CD-ROM.

VIRTUAL REALITY LABS, INC.

VistaPro

2341 Ganador Court
San Luis Obispo, CA 93401
805 545-8515

A landscape and terrain program.

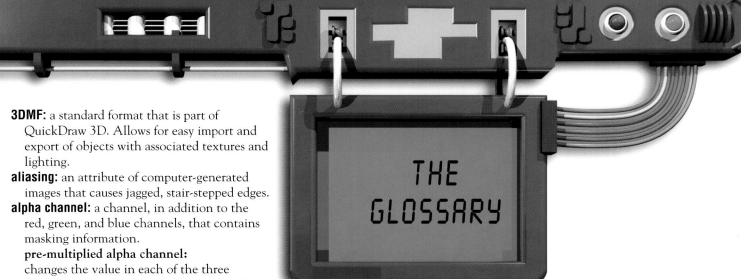

3DMF: a standard format that is part of QuickDraw 3D. Allows for easy import and export of objects with associated textures and lighting.

aliasing: an attribute of computer-generated images that causes jagged, stair-stepped edges.

alpha channel: a channel, in addition to the red, green, and blue channels, that contains masking information.

    pre-multiplied alpha channel: changes the value in each of the three (R,G,B) channels without adding a fourth channel.

    straight alpha channel: incorporates a separate (fourth) channel to handle transparency and masking information.

ambient light: the overall color and intensity of the light in a scene.

anti-aliasing: a program process required to remove the stair-step or jagged edges created when one object ends and another begins. Can be accomplished by blurring or blending the image edges together to get rid of the hard, jagged edge.

averaging: an anti-aliasing method. Averaging is a render output technique applied to an already rendered animation in QuickTime or PICS format. Each frame is analyzed and edges with high contrast are blurred together to remove the stair-stepping. While this method is faster than anti-aliasing, the results tend to be less crisp and precise than anti-aliasing.

backgrounds: the tangible and precise images used to enhance or give meaning to a scene.

Bezier curves: a graphical tool that allows users to precisely edit paths by adjusting the tangent of an arc, usually by clicking and dragging on handles.

Boolean operations: an operation that takes objects and uses the information from one object to add to or subtract from another object, resulting in a single new shape. The subtractive process is not so much a carving out as it is a molding—where one shape defines or redefines another. When joining two objects, the result allows the two shapes to share a seamless texture map.

central processing unit (CPU): either the little chip that runs the machine or the main box into which you plug monitor(s), keyboard, CD-ROM, and so forth.

color:

    depth: a measurement defined by the amount of information per pixel.

    RGB files: the Red, Green, Blue—usually used in video.

CMYK files: the Cyan, Magenta, Yellow and Black—usually used in print.

CODEC: compression/decompression used to reduce file size.

CPU: see central processing unit.

deformations: altering the shape of an object by twisting, stretching, scaling or bending.

depth setting: see recursion.

dithering option: allows normally smooth graduated tones to simulate the graduation by using dots for tonal change instead of the banding.

Drawing Exchange Format or File (DXF): image import and export format developed by AutoDesk and used by most modeling programs.

ease-in: accelerates movement slowly or naturally by adding more frames at the beginning of the sequence.

ease-out: decelerates movement slowly or naturally by adding more frames at the end of a sequence.

effects switcher: performs transitional effects—like dissolves—as the video from one deck switches to the other deck.

Encapsulated Postscript (EPS): an image import/export format for saving images created in a drawing program.

event mark or events: the changes that take place on the time line. See also key frames.

environments: the influence of everything that reflects light in your scene. Objects with some degree of reflectivity will give the feeling that the images are within an environment.

extruded shape: the depth given to a 2D form to create a 3D shape.

field render: the process that writes a frame for each odd and even layer of a video signal (for example, an image has 30 frames but 60 fields). The result is the smoothest possible animation.

fill light: a light source used to reduce the intensity of shadows and to keep unlighted areas of a scene from being too dark.

flat shading: a quick shading method that simply shades each polygon as its base color, regardless of reflections, transparencies or textures.

floating-point processors (FPU): the computation power that allows artists to create 3D artwork and animations on the computer. (Also known as math processors or math chips.)

frame: a single image.

frame recording: records a single frame of an animation at a time, one by one, to videotape. Allows for perfect quality and speed playback.

frame resolution : number of dots per inch (dpi) used in a single line of the image.
Standards for:
NTSC and computer screen resolution–72dpi
newsprint–160 dpi
magazines–220 dpi
books–300 dpi

gobos: the objects placed in front of a light source to create shadows.

Gouraud shading: rendering algorithm of a fast shading mode that allows smooth rendering and accurate lighting, but usually does not support texture maps or shadows.

graphic safe: for video or TV, the area within the NTSC window (640 pixels x 480 pixels) that incorporates the cropping from all sides (usually a half inch on all sides).

horizontal retrace: at the end of each horizontal line, the beam must return to the left side of the scene. Coordination of the horizontal retrace is handled by the horizontal sync pulse.

images: video images are normally RGB (Red, Green, Blue) files. Print images are usually CMYK (Cyan, Magenta, Yellow, and Black) files.

image imports/exports: are handled by five formats–QuickTime, PICT (PICT2), PICS, EPS, and DXF.

image map: applied to model surface.

in-betweening or tweening: computer calculation of an object's position between two points over a number of frames.

ink effects: influence how texture maps and layers are superimposed on other layers.

interlaced: video signals screen refresh or draws all odd lines, from top to bottom, then the even lines, top to bottom. See also non-interlaced.

jaggies: the very definite stair-stepped transitions between an art element and background.

key frames: a reference point in the time line where an event occurs.

linear event mark: an object travels in a direct path between event marks. Also called no spline control.

Lingo scripts: Macromedia Director's native scripting code that gives the user interactive control over what a movie is doing.

linking: physically connects one object with another. Links can pivot freely or be constrained. The relationship between objects is commonly referred to as child and parent. The child can move independently of the parent. When a parent moves, all child objects move.

mapping techniques: cubical, cylindrical, spherical, straight, and wrap.

metaballs: merge spherical shapes to create organic objects.

motion path: a path that represents an object's actions. Allows for accurate editing and instant feedback on an object's position.

non-interlaced: every line is refreshed sequentially, from top to bottom.

non-linear: the smoothness in which an object enters and leaves an event mark. Also called spline control.

NuBus cards: internally mounted cards provide self-contained improvement, such as acceleration, or provide a link for external devices, such as video cards.

numbered PICTS: a series of PICT files numbered sequentially.

NURBS: Non-uniform rational B-splines, a method of creating objects using a weighed spline resulting in smooth shapes.

orthographic mode: three viewing windows showing working area for the top, front and side.

parallel lights: a light source that acts as if it is coming from a distant point and not from a close central point like a spotlight.

Phong shading: rendering algorithm.

PICS: image import and export format. This is a file format that contains all the PICT frames of an animation. PICS does not allow compression methods like QuickTime, but keeps the quality of the image intact. Most animation programs and utilities support the PICS format.

PICT (PICT2): image import and export format.

pixelation: where the eye can detect individual pixels that make the image.

point lights: a light source emitting from a central point in space, radiating outwards in all directions.

primitives: elementary shapes that can be used when creating models.

procedural or volumetric maps and surfaces: computer-generated surface and color treatment that rely on mathematical algorithms rather than importing an image from an external file.

QuickTime: image import and export format. Apple's system extension combines video, sound and still image compression into a single package.

ramp: an audio term relating to sound volume.
ramp up: increase in sound.
ramp down: decrease in sound.

Random Access Memory (RAM): loaded into your RAM at any given time is the program you are using, your system program, a few extensions and control devices and your project data.

ray tracing: a realistic method of rendering that follows a ray of light from the camera lens out to the scene.

realtime recording: relies on hardware compression/decompression boards that send the video signal through the computer fast enough to display 30 frames a second.

realtime playback: ability to re-play an animation at the normal speed. Usually requires some type of acceleration for full-screen images.

recursion or depth setting:
for reflections: the number of times a reflection will bounce back and forth.
for transparencies: determines how many transparent objects you can look through before clear objects are no longer transparent.

reflection maps: reflection of objects can be controlled to make them slightly reflective or mirror-like.

rendering: computer takes the information the user has given it and converts it into the final image.

RIB format: a MacRenderMan format that can be used to transport files.

SCSI devices: system expansion that allows seven devices to be daisy-chained.

seamless textures: texture maps created so the opposite sides match each other, creating a seamless area when they are tiled together.

singular viewing plane or single world view: a single plane that allows the user to change quickly from top, bottom, front, side or a variable angle. The user moves around the model (changing views) via menu selection, navigational arrows, mouse manipulation or a virtual trackball. This system's advantage is that it allows the viewer to work with a single large window.

skinned objects: tool for creating irregular shapes by wrapping a skin over "ribs" to form a solid object. The ribs are usually a series of 2D shapes that have been edited to form an underlying structure.

spline control or curve: allow the motion at peak points to be smooth instead of sharply defined.

super-sampling: involves rendering a file several times larger than the size of the final image. Information from the larger image is used to better define the edges for the smaller, final image.

swept objects: tool for creating irregular shapes by taking the geometry of one shape—a circle—and making it follow the geometry of another form—a curved line. The result is a linear but irregular shape.

synchronize: for accurate reproduction, the video output card and the television receiver must be synchronized to scan the same part of the scene at the same time.

three-space: allows a modeler to view, simultaneously, a scene from three distinct viewing planes. This provides useful and immediate feedback on perceiving exactly what is going on from each vantage point.

tiled textures: small swatches of images, usually in PICT format, that when replicated side by side to cover an object, make a single seamless texture.

time line: reflects the different actions of objects over time.

tweening: see in-betweening.

visual retention: information transmitted from your eye to your brain in a manner that accounts for the transitions from one image to the next.

volumetric maps and surfaces: see procedural or volumetric maps and surfaces.

window size: video standards for NTSC require sizes that work out to be close to 640 pixels wide by 480 pixels deep. This is also the same size for a 13-inch computer screen. With the 640x480 window size set, a good portion of the edges of the animation will be chopped off—around 1/2 inch on all sides. Area within the non-chopped region is called graphic-safe, and must be planned for while the model and animation are being constructed.

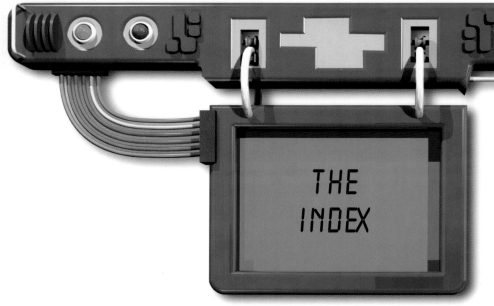

THE INDEX

ANIMATION
TIPS AND TRICKS
FOR WINDOWS AND MAC

BY DON AND MELORA FOLEY

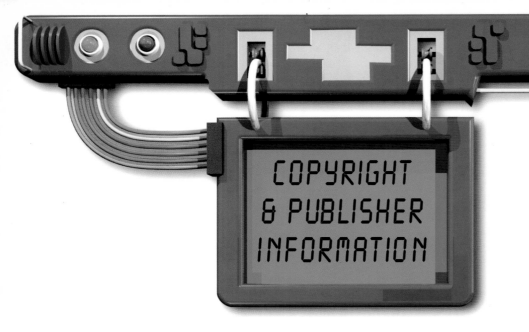

Animation Tips and Tricks for Windows and Mac
Don and Melora Foley

Peachpit Press
1249 8th Street
Berkeley CA 94710
510-524-2178
510-524-2221 (fax)

Find us on the World Wide Web at:
http://www.peachpit.com

Peachpit Press is a division of Addison-Wesley Publishing Company

Cover Design by Don Foley
Set in Goudy regular

ISBN- 0-201-69643-6

9 8 7 6 5 4 3 2 1

Manufactured in Hong Kong by Everbest Printing Company Ltd.